EYE OF THE BEHOLDER

THE INTERNATIONAL LIBRARY OF PHOTOGRAPHY

PICTURE.COM

Cara J. Griego, Editor

Eye Of The Beholder

Library of Congress
Cataloging in Publication Data

ISBN 1-58235-474-X

Printed in Hong Kong

Published by
The International Library of Photography
3600 Crondall Lane
Suite 101
Owings Mills, MD 21117

FOREWORD

Writing about photography is a difficult task, as it entails the translation of one art form into another. While every photograph may not inspire a thousand words, it is easy to see how the saying evolved. Words are a function of the intellect. But, much like music, a visual image speaks directly to the emotions, evoking an immediate and powerful response. Only when one attempts to analyze, interpret, and critique this image do words come into play.

As one views a photograph, one is slowly taken on a visual journey through the eye of the photographer. Whether the photograph was staged or the "point-and-click method" was employed, the picture represents the fact that moments in time pass within the blink of an eye. The photographer not only captures a scene or a subject; he also creates a lasting, tangible image of a fleeting instant. The beauty of photography is that any individual can produce an image of these passing moments.

Photography represents both an active and a passive art form. The degree to which a photographer participates in his art form varies from photograph to photograph. The photographer can either tell a story within the photograph, or simply stand aside and record life as it happens. The one thing that holds true for all photography is this: without the photographer there can be no photograph. Even in a simple snapshot, the photographer's influence is clearly evident.

The photographs within this anthology exhibit their own importance as well as demonstrate the importance of the photographer. In some cases, the idea or photo found the photographer. For instance, while taking pictures on a nature hike, a photographer may catch the sunset as it breaks through a bunch of trees, and thus an idea may be born. In other instances, a photographer may orchestrate and choreograph the set-up of a photograph in order to fulfill a creative idea or notion. (This may be the case in still-life or abstract photography.)

Another similar element in most of these photographs is the photographer's love of and dedication to his subject. For example, nature photography is often captured by devoted nature watchers. Those people who take humorous photographs usually enjoy the lighter side of life and tend to look for the funniest aspect of any situation. The numerous photographs of children in this book were most likely taken by parents or grandparents who appreciate the joy and wonderment contained in a child's smile. Becoming emotionally involved with a subject, through deep love or interest, often enables a photographer to generate ideas that help him capture the true essence of his subject.

There are also photographers who gain inspiration not from relating to one specific subject or another, but rather from focusing on the photographic process itself. They often use special techniques to create images they have envisioned within their own minds, or they choose to concentrate on one particular aspect of photography (such as lighting) and through experimentation examine its effect on a particular subject. By casting aside conventional approaches, these photographers open different pathways to new ideas, allowing their own imaginations to roam freely.

No matter how or why a photograph is taken, the viewer must realize that each photograph represents an individual's artistic viewpoint. There are many excellent photographs contained in this anthology. At a quick glance they might appear to be just pictures, but be sure to focus on the ideas being conveyed, both emotionally and physically. Allow yourself to become lost in the photo: perhaps you may gain a new understanding of it, or you may simply be able to relate more deeply to the photographer's viewpoint.

Andy Warhol once predicted that in the future everyone will have his fifteen minutes in the spotlight. This philosophy could easily be applied to photography by simply stating that every subject has its moment, and as a photographer, one must strive to find and capture these instants. After all, these cherished moments, which may seem frozen in time when we see them through the camera's viewfinder, do not last fifteen minutes; rather, viewing a photograph that captures these instances may trigger memories that will always remain embedded deep within our minds. Through photographs we are therefore offered a physical reminder as an accompaniment to a memory. We then hold in our hands the permanency of a cherished moment in time—an image of yesterday.

Russell Hall
Senior Editor

EDITOR'S NOTE

Artists of all mediums seek to convey ideas that seem natural to all people, no matter what their backgrounds are. Photographers avidly pursue natural looking pictures, ones that do not seem contrived or posed, so that we admire their skill in capturing an image that only lasted for a few moments. The ability to be mindful of what is around you, or of the person or place you are photographing, is a valuable skill. It is a quality that helps make a photograph fascinating to view. If an image is natural, a person viewing it has a better chance of relating to it or identifying with some aspect of it. A person might particularly enjoy a photograph of a child running through a sprinkler in the summertime because their own child used to do the same thing, but they never got a picture. Photographs can become universal images that never lose meaning.

Sadly, we live in a world advancing so swiftly that a great amount of the remarkable images it has had to offer can never be seen again. There are many endangered animals, and some have even become extinct. Ancient trees have been cut down and landscapes destroyed for the sake of progress and industrialization. Future photographs have been preemptively removed from this world. This is not to say that what mankind has created is not worthy of art. In the realm of photography, man-made subjects can reveal as much clarity and meaning as a nature photograph. It is unfortunate that the relationship between man and nature often feels antagonistic, as if the two cannot coexist. Even then, a skilled photographer can capture that conflict to raise awareness in others. Even with so much of our natural world tainted, photographers still find natural images to inspire and impress us. Whether the photograph is of nature, or simply an unposed, natural picture of a person, these pure images can convey truth and emotion.

The Grand Prize winning photograph, "Teressa, Look At Me!," by George I. Antar, does a beautiful, colorful job of showing a child in a very natural way-having fun. One gets the impression that the child, Teressa, was in the midst of playing outside, possibly in a kiddie-pool filled with bubbles, when the photographer yelled out the title of the picture to get her attention. Suds are dripping down her face, off her chin, and all over her body. Teressa's pause for the photographer was probably a short moment of surprise, lasting only a moment when she heard her name. Most likely, she jumped right back into the pool to play, not thinking much about having her portrait taken in such an honest fashion. Perhaps she was playing in her back yard with a friend who is off camera. She has a very serious expression on her face, perhaps a part of the surprise from being called to by Antar. Maybe she thought she was in trouble when she heard her name. Or she might simply have been intrigued by the camera focusing in on her.

Antar used an interesting technique called shallow depth of field, to affect the feeling of the photograph. Teressa appears to almost float, disjointed from the background of the photograph, which is blurred and swirled. One can see the colorful pat-

tern of the kiddie-pool behind her, but the images are hazy and blended together. The outline of Teressa's figure looks like it is laid on top of a movie blue-screen, because it is so crisp and distinct. She is the exact opposite of the background—extremely detailed and clear; the bubbles of the suds glisten in the sun, and her bathing suit is extremely eye-catching and bright. The yellow ruffles immediately captures the viewer's attention. What is most important is that this photo realistically portrays a child playfully engaged in something fun and exciting. The picture does not seem posed. It is merely a pause in the activity she was enthralled with. Like an animal in the wild, a child in the midst of playing is a beautiful, natural thing.

"Mt. Kilimanjaro And Beyond," by Lisa S. Reed, takes us to the untouched beauty of the African landscape. Reed's photograph is very grand in scope, with the looming presence of Mt. Kilimanjaro in the background with a blanket of clouds

around it. The mountain is far in the distance, but its size is still impressive. Reed framed the picture in such a way that we realize the mountain's scope, but at the same time it does not detract from the magnificent elephant in the foreground. Much like Teressa in the midst of playing, this elephant looks as if it was in the process of walking or eating, and paused to observe the photographer or the car she is in. The lone elephant looks so calm, almost thoughtful against the vast background. This is definitely not a mindless creature, it is a majestic animal whose very nature is beautiful.

The color in the photograph is actually very interesting, although not as glaringly bright as Teressa's bathing suit in the Grand Prize winning photo. It appears

Reed took this photograph either very early in the morning, or around dusk. At first the color appears slightly dull, but in reality it is just the cool lighting given off when the sun is not at its zenith. This avoids the look that pictures often get in bright lighting—the appearance that the subject is obviously being singled out. This gives it a more natural look. The sky is a soft blue, the clouds are delicate and blend into the haze around the mountain, and the ground has hints of pink and purple. This lighting gives the photograph a soft, consistent, almost painting-like quality. Reed's image does a tremendous job of showing us a remarkable, truly natural subject, untouched by man or technology.

Philosophically, man has a very complex relationship with nature. At times, it seems we live in harmony and mankind respects the natural world. However, it is not rare for the situation to seem much more antagonistic. We have sacrificed so much of what nature has to offer us for the progress of our culture, for technology, and for personal gain. Sometimes man seems more natural in that which he has created, since everyday life for a human relies more on the products of our technology than nature.

"Fare Play" by Nancy Hoffman is a photograph of a man, doubly inside his own creations–in a car, in a city. The man is visible in the driver's seat of the taxi, with the city around him distorted and blurred. The effect the photographer used creates the

feeling of movement. The picture makes it seem like the taxi is coming towards us. We get the feeling of impending doom, as if the taxi is actually going to hit us. However, the blurry background also gives us a feeling of discomfort and confusion in the city. There is nothing distinguishable in the background of this photograph; the buildings have all become gray lines. The photographer seems to be portraying the urban setting as a place where nothing is distinct or clear. The man driving the car is anonymous; his features are barely visible through the windshield. We wonder very little about him because he is so underplayed in the composition of the photograph. The surroundings become more important in the visual aspect of the photograph. Man seems very insignificant when surrounded by the overwhelming products of our society.

As much as we focus on the differences between mankind and nature, sometimes a photographer can capture a picture that alters our view completely. A poignant image can show the love some people still have towards the natural world. Thomas C. Ming Jr. successfully combines the natural and human world in an image that shows us how delicate both can be together and how they can still coexist peacefully in his photograph, "Prince Charming." The hand in which the tiny frog rests looks very gentle and caring. The woman is holding the frog so lightly that it probably could jump away if it wanted to. The woman's arm fades into the background of the photo; only

her hand is clearly in focus with the frog. This gives the feeling of a distinct center to the photograph. The viewer can pick out the tiny details of the frog's skin. At the same time, we can see the delicate wrinkles on the woman's hand and knuckles. The more one looks at the images, the more the frog and hand seem like one entity, not two distinct parts. This quality is enhanced by the color of the image, a distinct black-and-white style, which makes the picture look very old and monotone. Ming Jr. conveys the feeling that there is little difference between man and nature, and we can live in harmony, respecting each other's significance in the world.

Natural photography is a very gratifying art, one that requires patience and timing to capture animals, landscapes, or people in their most honest and inspiring moment. Some of these photographs are great examples of the beauty in nature and its relationship to man, while others are skillfully captured images of people doing what they naturally are inclined to do. There is a respectable honesty to these images, and the photographers who took them have a definite vision of this world.

I would like to thank the entire staff at The International Library of Photography for all of their time and assistance. This book would not have been possible without the hard work of the judges, editors, administrative services staff, customer service representatives, data entry personnel, office administrators, computer service staff, and mail room staff. Congratulations and thanks to all of the photographers who contributed their work, and good luck in all of your future endeavors.

Gregory P. Rago
Editor

Grand Prize Winner

George I. Antar
Teressa, Look At Me!

Children

Karen C. Bowman   Children
The Boy And The Puppy

Ralph Blackburn   Sports
Basket Of Smiles

Timothy Ardroudi   Travel
A Castle In My Dream

Linda Stahl   Animals/Pets
Casper The Dream Catcher

Cheryl Briant Srnka   Portraiture
Grandma

Cristiany Rabelo   Travel
Le Plateau Mont - Royal

Steve Kuhn   Other
Old Bathroom

Luke Galambos   People
Dramatic Mask

Ed Gerber   Humor
Knight And Today

Charles M. Sullivan   Action
Las Vegas Motor Speedway

Lisa Creedon   Animals/Pets
Best Buddies

Lorraine Pecnick   Other
Zeb's Finest!

Jennifer Sorrentino Nature
Dewdrops On Pumpkin Leaves

Susan R. Meiler Humor
Snoozing

Bryan Gill Animals/Pets
Happiness At Feeding Time

Scott Blatt Animals/Pets
Leopard In A Tree

Annette Czupylo People
Cuna Indian Woman

Lindsey P. Martin Travel
Lighthouse Reflection, Peggy's Cove

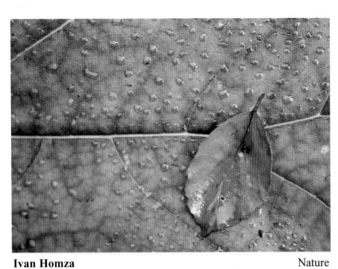

Ivan Homza   Nature
Still Life

Joe Meyer   People
Street Show

Ron Cooper   Other
Gorgeous Georgian

Maria Guadalupe Acosta Peña   People
Sin Titulo

Luis Ramos   Portraiture
Untitled

Chris Henry   Portraiture
Version 2.37

Virginia Connors   Other
The Sewing Basket

Ricardo Coral   People
Pager

Rose Bromberg   Sports
Sunday Riding

A. Boyd   Children
Concentration

Joseph R. Sedlacek   Animals/Pets
Owls Are You?

John Severino   Animals/Pets
Wanna Play?

Daniel Sawyer People
The Chief

Linda Kimmel Children
Morgan And Henri

Johnise Dupree Portraiture
Exhale

Dave Brotherton Children
Batter Up

Sebastiano Stia Jr. Travel
Simpler Times

Kady Jackson People
Kenmore Square Musician

Joe Quayle Other
Untitled

Michele Fairchild Animals/Pets
Jumping Dolphins

Martha Mirosh Animals/Pets
Our Dog, Flag

Julie Vicari Animals/Pets
Want A Treat?

Dede Myers Children
Fall Festival

Karen Feinberg Animals/Pets
Sorry, Vegetarians Only

Noal K. Hatch Travel
Utah Lake

Una Smith Sports
Yo Ho-Ho

Jim Deeds Sports
Ice Adventure

Sherri Booz Travel
Hope

Temeka Prioleau Children
Untitled

Christine Ward Travel
Inspiring View Of Giotto Bell Tower

Barbara Eckelhoff   Children
Fish Story

Elaine A. Newberg   Children
Innocence Of Spring

Thomas C. Ming Jr.   Nature
Prince Charming

Amanda Martin   Other
Closed For Business

Judy Barrows   Humor
Sharing

Darwin Eicher   Sports
The Phantom Bat And Ball

Jane H. Marsh   Nature
Southeastern Lubber Grasshopper

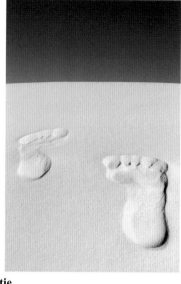

Robert Christie   Other
Mark On History

Christian J. Español   People
Petra Reyes—Venezuelan Indian

Halina Krymuza   People
Pottery Maker

Joseph K. Gordon   Animals/Pets
In Flight

Christina J. Gallagher   Travel
Montmarte

Katie Wade   Portraiture
Enlightenment

Steven Presbury   Travel
Thai Monastery

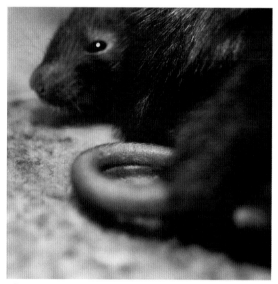

Susan Inverso   Animals/Pets
Tail, Nose, Eyes

Judy Erickson   Nature
Look At Me

Aleene Tran   Other
Untitled

Amy McGee   Other
Time Stands Still

Dorothy Reno   Children
Swing For Success

Earl Carswell   Other
Some Like It Hot

Emma Murphy   Travel
Coliseum At Night

André H. Samson   Children
The Red Turban

Ila Reber   Animals/Pets
A Pale Horse

Carla Maloco   Animals/Pets
The Highlanders

Michelle Velasco   Portraiture
Untitled

Richard Duerksen   Action
Cooling Off

Ziny Flikop   Animals/Pets
Warrior

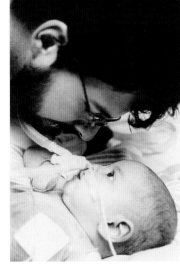

Michele Hermsen   People
Transplant Eve

Nancy Hoffman   Travel
Fare Play

Steven Troast   Animals/Pets
Yellowstone Gray Wolf

Todd A. Mulligan   Other
Voluminous Veggies

Tracy Foertsch   Travel
Shanghai Street Corner

Sherri Dearden   Humor
Daisy—Swimming

Yun Ying Du   Children
Curiosity

David Ferguson   Animals/Pets
Up And Over

Steve Wideen   Sports
Intensity

Ben Shulok   Portraiture
She

Hyung S. Kim   Action
Untitled

Lawrence R. Gruss   Travel
Span Of Light

John C. Rjabak   Sports
The Pre-Race Race

Autumn Morrice   Children
Our Children, Our Future

Rodolfo Alexandre B. Tardin   Animals/Pets
Brazil

Tara Fairfield   Humor
Public Drinking Fountain

Margaret W. Sprott   Nature
Fall Reflections I

Angela Matthews   Portraiture
Mask

Sean Kramber   Action
Misty Water

Penny Starr   Portraiture
My Niece's Wedding

Kara Fordney   Other
Human Statue

Sal Moley　　　　　　　　　　　　　　People
Joyful Jan

Caroline Witko　　　　　　　　　　　Children
A Sip

Tracey Holloway　　　　　　　　Animals/Pets
The Desert Tortoise

R. D. Larson　　　　　　　　　　　Nature
A New Day

Alesia A. Johnson　　　　　　　Animals/Pets
DJ

George I. Antar　　　　　　　　　Children
Teressa, Look At Me!

David J. Tecci   Humor
Push Me, Pull You

James P. Zamenick   Travel
Wing's Castle

Diana Stacey   Nature
Beauty And The Beast

Lisa S. Reed   Nature
Mount Kilimanjaro And Beyond

Keiko O. Case   Other
Park Bench In Fall

Sandra Hammaker   Portraiture
Smile

Gene Niederhaus   Animals/Pets
The Rider

Robert Pflumm   Sports
There

Melissa Aiello   People
Melanie

Julia Davis   Portraiture
Emily

Janos Bingham   Nature
Red-Tailed Hawk Of Monroe County

Lori Borchert   Portraiture
Stephanie

Lisa Criselle — People
How Big Was That Fish?

Carrie M. Abbuhl — Nature
God's Handiwork

Ruth Minnich — Children
Looking For Trouble

Cathy Watts — Children
Mom, How Do I Look?

Mary Pachinakis — Nature
Sunset

Marla Messer McCowan And Randy Voth — Nature
Blue Beauty In Prince William Sound

Engelberto G. Gammad   Other
Silence And Solitude

Laura Garrison   Nature
Morning Glory At Yellowstone

Darrin F.   Nature
Bull Canyon

Mary Janik   Animals/Pets
Making A Splash

Michele Walat   Animals/Pets
Afternoon Reflections

Elizabeth P. White   Animals/Pets
King Of The Mountain

Anne Wix   Animals/Pets
Blissfully Asleep

Ashley Fraser   Travel
Australia's People

Kathleen Hoye   Children
Untitled

Dave Lawlor   Animals/Pets
Eve

Eva Miller   Animals/Pets
Cookie

Marie Tuvi-Uthe   Nature
Nature's Diamond

Darla Hunt   People
My Halloween Baby

Connie Scaccia   Children
First Meeting

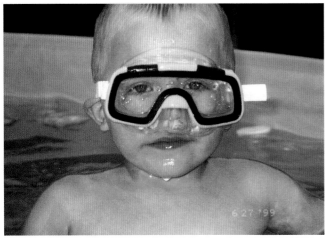

Holly Spier   Children
The Fish, Tommy

Barbara Patz   Children
Mirror, Mirror

George Radoumis   Animals/Pets
Handsome Rusty

Alexis Fincik   People
Sweet Innocence

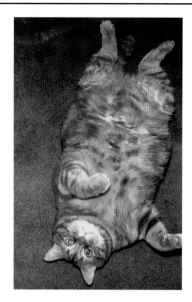

Freda Hale Animals/Pets
Laid Back

Ann M. Bishop Children
First Kiss

A. I. Hines Children
Champ

Fred Testa Nature
Why Me, Lord?

Janese Herren People
Chuck Herren

Frieda M. Hall People
Like Mother, Like Daughter

Elizabeth Reed Animals/Pets
Morning Gossip Over The Fence

Patt T. Pappas Nature
Sunrise On Perdido Bay

Jett Carman Children
Happy Days Are Here Again

William Knowles Animals/Pets
Disco Kids

Doris K. Perfetto Nature
Top Of The Rockies

Leigh Peet Children
Lost Potato Chip

27

Caitlyn Hartzog   Children
Got Milk?

Mary A. Ligos   Children
My Best Friend

Delia Nuffer   Animals/Pets
We Want Out Too

Jennifer Potter   Animals/Pets
Marcellus Wallace

Denise Gionet   Nature
Summer's Majesty

Valerie Crandall   Nature
Early Morning Pelican

Virginia L. Kimmel　　　　Animals/Pets
Miles, Tell Me Another Joke!

Barbara Fogle　　　　Nature
Northwest Territory

June McLean　　　　Animals/Pets
Who's A Mama's Boy?

Wendy Lee Prato　　　　Nature
Sunrise At The Shore

Susan A. Dodson　　　　Nature
Sunset On Flathead Lake

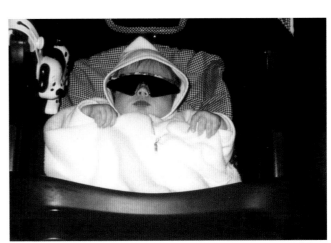

Holly Walker And Barbara Miller　　　　Children
My Future's So Bright, I Gotta Wear Shades!

Cynthia Kyelberg Children
Awestruck!

Wynarda Erguiaga People
It Must Have Been Good!

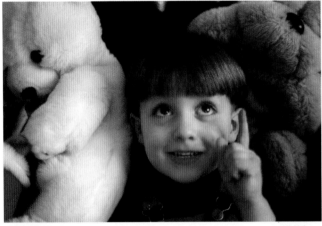

Elizabeth Stark Children
A Christmas Gift

Ileene Lorimer Other
Summer Fun And Illusion

Debra J. Heckler Animals/Pets
Duchess The Dog, Stealing Money

Sarah Aldrich Travel
Boating In Maine

Rhonda Williams   Travel
Piece Of Heaven—Georgia

Carla Blomseth   Nature
Colorado Blue

Donna Vitina   Children
Wash Day

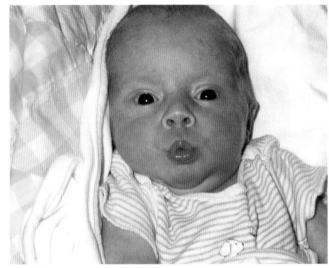

Alice Page   Children
After A Yawn

Lori Khile   Children
Ball Anyone?

Jaime Stellek-Browne   Animals/Pets
Hurry, Take The Picture

Peggy O'Connell   Children
Princess Devin's Private Moment

Ethel G. Burton   Nature
Sunset On The Pamunkey River

Gale L. Foca   Nature
Acadia National Park, ME

Adrienne M. Harter   Nature
Beauty Found In The Aftermath

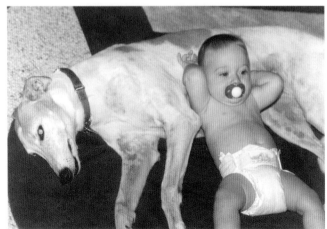

Charmaine Harris   Children
Life Is Good

Mary L. Scolaro   Animals/Pets
Buck Loves Grandpa!

Wendy Cooper   People
New Mother And Child

Kia R. Baker   Children
Watermania

Shirley A. Bean   Other
The Beauty Of Sunrise

Terry Davis   Nature
Ice Needles

Margaret S. Ellett   Animals/Pets
You Woke Me Up!

Maureen Dimont   Travel
Burano, Italy

Versa B. Parnell   Children
Feeding The Fish

Mirian Farley   Children
Lounging On The Lawn

Jonny Howell   Children
Halloween, Hula Girl

Bernard A. Williams   Portraiture
Love Blooms

Mariano Santiago   Animals/Pets
Jazz And Her Favorite Frisbee

Robert Breit   People
I'm The Man, Vote For Me

Denise Mikesh   Children
Slick Willy

Lynn Barrett   Children
Having A Ball

Twana Langley   Children
Merry Christmas

Mary Rider   Nature
Winter In Wisconsin

Melva Carnival   Other
Meet My Friend!

Gladys Brown   Nature
Cunningham Park

Betty Anderson   Nature
Look At You

Raymond Chen   Travel
Harbor Girl

Kelly Zandi   Nature
Red Sky In The Morning

Betty Todd   People
Nap Time

Will McGrath   Other
Moon At Night

Lydia Elsenraat   Animals/Pets
I Like It In Here

Kelly M. Higgins   Animals/Pets
Funny Bunny

Sharon Farrell   Children
Can't Play Today

Ramona Tart Beasley   Nature
Carolina Sunset

Catherine M. Bond   Children
Landscaping—My Little Helper

Harold Scharf   Children
Big Sister With New Brother

Phyllis Davis Moore   Nature
Cooper's Rock

Mary Hull   Humor
Oh, La La, Look What I've Laid!

Barbara Sprong   People
Cousins: High School Graduation

Margo Scott   Animals/Pets
The Squirrel Patrol

Carolyn Rodish-Sims   Children
Beach Baby

Yvonne Gordon   Animals/Pets
Cody

Jerome Barrette   Nature
Winter Wonderland

Jane Stumpf   Other
Two Babies

Gina M. Rizzuto   Children
Oodles Of Noodles

Rebecca A. Snyder   Nature
Sunrise

Jack Carter   Animals/Pets
A Don King Look-A-Like

Marion Gould   Nature
Warm Summer Day

Jenna Parsons   Travel
The Wilmington, NC, Sky

La Verne McDonnell   Children
Cuddle Time

Linda Tranum   Animals/Pets
Whispering Sweet Nothings

Brenda J. Silva   Children
Nathaniel's First Pumpkin

Mitzi Sequoia   Nature
The Cocoon

Steven Harold Simpson   Action
The Balloon Dive Toss

Angie Homer   Nature
Golden Splendor

Garrett Sean Hug — Nature
Evening Pleasure

Emily Spahn — Other
Don't Fence Me In

Erika Franolich — Animals/Pets
Quality Time

Cassy Lake — Nature
Sunset On The Lake

Arlene Parker — Nature
Sunrise

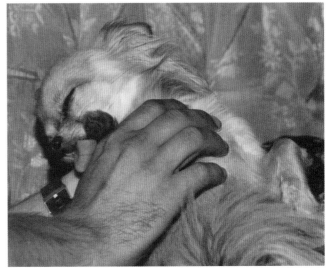

Carol Thompson — Animals/Pets
Unconditional Love

Joseph Martin   Children
Warrior

Gloria Pazik   Children
Proof That Eating Makes You Sleepy

Laura Chao Huneycutt   Nature
Sun's Rays

Megan J. Metzger   Nature
The Japanese Gardens

Linda Ingram   Other
Room With A View

Gregg Vilkaitis   Animals/Pets
Sleeping In Sunshine

42

Susan E. Craley　　　　　　　　　　People
My First Fishing Trip

Hilal Derbentli　　　　　　　　　　Other
Tolerance

Bree Bishop　　　　　　　　　　Animals/Pets
Say What?

Elizabeth Hebbe　　　　　　　　　　Animals/Pets
The Last Lazy Days Of Fall

Robert Paul Wright　　　　　　　　　　People
Le Femme Impersonaire

Karen Coburn　　　　　　　　　　Other
Japanese Serenity

Rosella Jessen   Portraiture
Birdhouse Village

Dennis G. Miller   People
Doo Dah Truta

Stacey Smith   Travel
Fall

Robin J. Brassfield   Animals/Pets
She Has To Share

Barbara Allgeo   Children
Ready To Ride

Paul E. Brent   Other
Bayhorse Ghost Town

Octavia Vaughan   Nature
Bridal Veil

Virginia Gibson   People
Mr. Burnett Turned Ninety-Nine

Tere Conroy   Sports
Yankees Stadium, Here We Come

Christine McCarthy   Travel
California Wines

Irwin G. Lander   People
Queen Of Beads And Her Elves

Gina Short Friedman   Animals/Pets
In The Company Of Dogs

Neil Herrick   Children
Boy Swimming

Barbara De Waal   People
Hooray! Graduation Day

Fred Sandoval   Travel
In Awe

Judy Boyer   Nature
Dogwood In Ice

Pam Gwin   Other
Buckingham Fountain

Byron Hatfield   Children
Child, Cowboy Boots, Hat

Teresa Fedak Animals/Pets
Puppy Love

Lynn Robinson Children
Good Girl, Lady Bell

Marie I. Clark Animals/Pets
Beauty At Its Best

Barbara Corstange Animals/Pets
On The Alert

Maureen R. Gervais Nature
Autumn's Beauty

Carolyn Sue Hauter Portraiture
Beautiful Bride

Paulette George   Animals/Pets
Bring On The Snow!

Adeline Kroc   Nature
Yosemite Gold

Betty Keith   Animals/Pets
Angels In A Cloud

Fran Wines   Children
Sisterly Love

Mary Jane Brandt   Nature
Peaceful Meal

Ann Holthoff   People
Celebrate

Sandra L. Souza　　　　　　　　　　　Other
Intrigued

Suzanne Kidder　　　　　　　　　　　Children
End Of Summer

Sandra A. Martin　　　　　　　　　　Nature
Winter's Magic

Hal M. Buchanan　　　　　　　　　Animals/Pets
Dad's Helper?

Sarah Wallace　　　　　　　　　　　Nature
Trust

Jackie Shaw　　　　　　　　　　　Children
Jenna's Joy

Mary Mae Head Action
Dog Drinking

Bill Phelps Children
Anna's Bubble

Dianne Chmidling Children
Amish Cousins

Matt Roesch Other
Time Passing By The Eternal Moments

Robin Deakins Portraiture
Shannon In Bloom

Larry Stormes Travel
El Trovar At The Rim

Gianni Messina   Nature
Tranquil

Janet T. Ford   Sports
Father And Son Rules Of The Game

Virginia Francis   Animals/Pets
Here Comes Trouble!

James M. FitzGerald   Nature
Doomed

Frank Spinnato   Travel
Venice

Joseph D. Schreck   Nature
Tropical Moonrise

Lisa McGill   Children
Baby Love

Jessica Ruhlig   Children
Curious Together

Mark L. Peterson   Travel
Tribute To Walter Payton

Michael E. Bowman   Children
Halloween Wonder

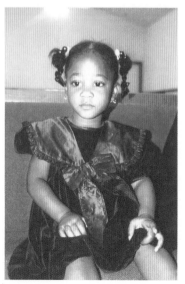

Rosa Jordan   People
Captivating Innocence

Lee Burris   Nature
First Light

Peggy Scaggs   Children
Cowboy Caleb

Nancy Rahz   Other
Ascending To Heaven

De Hou Yang   Portraiture
Old Woman

Denise Warren   Portraiture
Innocence

Mark Vogt   Animals/Pets
Legacy

Murry M. Kachel   Children
Sister And Baby Brother

Dee Brown　　　　　　　　　　　　　　　　　Nature
The Gate

David Schafer　　　　　　　　　　　　　　　Nature
Lone Juniper

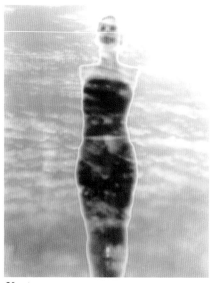

Douglas E. Kurtz　　　　　　　　　　　　　Other
Mon Ange

George Liskow　　　　　　　　　　　　　　Nature
Antelope Canyon

Cynthia S. Phillips　　　　　　　　　　Animals/Pets
The Pelican

Gary F. Joye　　　　　　　　　　　　　　　People
Playing For Pesos

Jean B. Foster　　　　　　　　　　Nature
Pasture Pest

Gary C. White　　　　　　　　　　Other
Sunset

Dean C. King　　　　　　　　　　Other
Bridge On University Pond

Debra Dietrich　　　　　　　　　　Nature
Golden Cottonwood

Chris Sliwa　　　　　　　　　　Children
Now What Am I Going To Do!

Diann Haglund　　　　　　　　　　Children
Innocence At The Fair

Carolyn Schaefer   Children
I Found My Pumpkin!

Mindi Sanchez Black   Animals/Pets
Basketful Of Sweetness

Robert F. Spencer   Animals/Pets
Anybody Home?

Carl Bowman   People
Best Friends Cutting Up

Amie Davis   Children
Sibling Love

Joy Turner   Animals/Pets
Lucky's Dream World

Sabra Close　　　　　　　　　　　　　Animals/Pets
Pleasant Perch

Sharon J. Roberts　　　　　　　　　　Children
Bride With Flower Girls

Marillyn Hale　　　　　　　　　　　　Animals/Pets
Contemplation

Gary Sneck　　　　　　　　　　　　　Animals/Pets
Best Friends

Flora Plasencia　　　　　　　　　　　Animals/Pets
This Is The Life

Rayna Regenthal　　　　　　　　　　Animals/Pets
Rottweiler Taking A Running Dive

Rebecca W. Powers   Humor
Puppet On A String

Marolyn McCormick   Action
Infinity

Kim Vescovi   Nature
West Virginia Winter

Daisy Cordell   Children
Precious Moments Last A Lifetime

Cynthia Griffing   Portraiture
Clown Fest '98

Elise Harrison   Other
Gifts Of A Lifetime

Leo F. Dooley   Animals/Pets
Time For A Nap

Tracey Watts   Children
Beechbums

Rachel Lieman   Nature
Concord River

Lucy M. Fisher   Children
Happy Grandchild, I'm Okay

Sarah Beaver   Nature
Nature's Perfect Pattern

Deborah Lacy   Nature
Springtime In Arkansas

Barbara Stephen
An Autumn Day

People

H. Matthews
Calling The White House

Children

Nan Iselin
A New Beginning

Nature

Pat Nelson
Tah-Dah, I Think I'm Full!

Children

Doris A. Stevens
Darling Tessi

Animals/Pets

Olga Miller
Niagara Falls

Travel

Melissa Grossman — Children
Riley

Amy R. Mansfield — Animals/Pets
Maximan

Staggers — Animals/Pets
Santa's Helpers

Kay Maring — Animals/Pets
Open The Gate

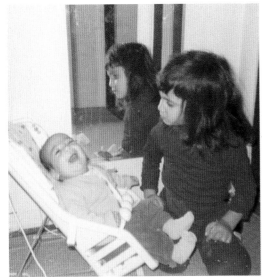

Sylvia Zagha — Children
Reflections Of Youth

Linda Pullin — Children
Western Bath

Carol Lane　　　　　　　　　　　　Children
Mi Amigo

Ann Marie Malone　　　　　　　　Animals/Pets
Jax's First Birthday

Karen Peters　　　　　　　　Animals/Pets
Corey And Spock

Maria Elena Perez　　　　　　Animals/Pets
Tara On The Mailbox

Nancy E. Bouch　　　　　　　　Humor
My Husband Plastering A Wall

Gaby Vargas　　　　　　　　Travel
Historical Street

Theresa L. Safrit   Nature
Sunset

Phyllis Jakubac   Nature
Autumn Colors

Tracey Benjamin   Children
Cheese

Mary C. Hall   Sports
Race You Back

Richard Gunther   Animals/Pets
Sleepy Heads

Tara Gushock   Animals/Pets
Christian Carrying A Bag

Marie Seubert   Animals/Pets
Sisters

Colette Marais   Animals/Pets
Abby

Alise Perkins   Animals/Pets
Tails Up

Diane Hovan   Animals/Pets
What Should I Do?

Kimberly Kelly   Animals/Pets
Hide And Seek

Crystal Wimmers   Nature
Home Tweet Home

Jeff Grossman Other
The Old Fisherman Of Crete

Larry Weddington Travel
Blue Ridge Park, Mabrys Mill

Betty Marshall Nature
Autumn In The Country

Alfred W. Gray Travel
Chateau Azay-Le-Rideau

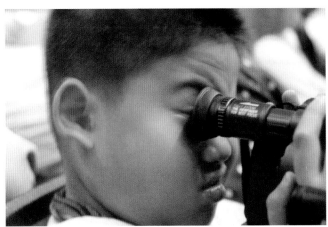

Marcelo Gayahan Children
I See It

Tom Kral People
Old Friends Full Bloom

Yan Gilbert   Nature
Silhouettes Of The Evening

Mary Gagliardi   Sports
Determination

Karin Porter   Children
Making Hay While The Sun Shines

Marge Heilman   Children
My Secret Recipe

Herman Wong   Nature
Triple Butterfly

Anne Kimberly Moore   Animals/Pets
Gizmo

Jacqueline Castellini   Nature
We All Have A Path In Life To Choose

Josh Bryant   Nature
Lotus

Ron Van Sickle   Animals/Pets
Soakin' Up The Sun

Cheri Gehlen   Humor
Ha Ha, Maggie, Ha Ha

Colleen Ferreri   Nature
Clouds

Patricia Copper   Nature
Majestic Moment

Frances K. Kirby   People
Dad And Daughter At Coolidge Water Park

Lou Vincent   Children
Keely

Peggy Poynter   Other
Best Friends

Eva Marie Butler   Children
My Worm

Palmira Marando   Children
Nana's Treasures!

Kristin Howell   Animals/Pets
Winkin, Blinkin, And Nod

Tammie Boisjoli Nature
Keukenhof Gardens

Wendy Hallett People
Nana And I've Had A Long Day

Susan Tramp Animals/Pets
Ricki Waiting

Joanne M. Szuflita Animals/Pets
Yes, Dear!

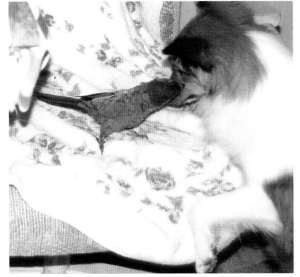

Geraldine Jankowski Animals/Pets
Hold Still, Just Checking

Jennifer Reese Other
Riverside Fountain

Diana Meszaros   Animals/Pets
Is This My Grub, Or Yours?

Velda Stahlecker   Nature
Prairie Sunset

Tammy Smith   Animals/Pets
Not Heads, But Tails

Edna Zimmerman   Children
Look At My Fish

Julie Billings   Nature
Face To The Sun

Amber Johnston   Animals/Pets
Walk This Way

Kevin Burdeshaw Children
Bathing With Lily

Jeremy Witmer Nature
On The Road To A Beautiful Sunrise

Marie Adkins Animals/Pets
Coco, My Beautiful Big Friend

Catherine Hartman Nature
Family Forest

Lynn Clark Nature
Getting Close

Gerald Marnell Animals/Pets
4-H Bucket Calf Project

Normalee R. Steele   Nature
Worshiping At The Great Frog God

Beverly Smith   Nature
Escape

Martha Faltisco   Children
Neil Having Breakfast With Santa And Friends

Donald S. Cohan   Humor
Does She Believe This Man?

Elizabeth M. Hutchins   Nature
A Plane View Of Mount Ranier

Richard F. Whitford   Nature
Reflections

Halina Zygmunt Janiak   Children
Untitled

Natalie Bucci   Nature
Coast Of Maine

Sabrina Balthazor   Nature
Stepping Upward

Mary Bowen   Animals/Pets
At Leisure, Beginner's Lucky Star

Janice L. Hechler   Other
Urban Sunrise

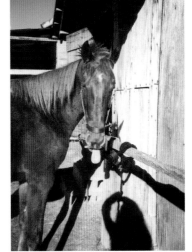

Amy Hearn   Animals/Pets
Horse With An Attitude

Dorothy J. Borger Animals/Pets
I Finally Have My Own Chair—This Is My Chair!

Tula Gounaris Children
Peaceful Moments

La Donna Strain Other
Indian Sunset

Joan S. Spofford Children
Lesson

Mario Savoca Nature
Peaceful Fields

Sherri VanSickle Children
Hangin' Out On An Autumn Day

Harry K. Zaharko   Nature
Morning Light

Joan E. Dreier   Children
Mudder's Little Helper

Debra Ann Rouse   People
Lunch In The Park

Brian L. Stevenson   Nature
Fish Creek On Denali Highway Near Cantwell, AK, With Talkotna Mtns.

Kathryn White   Nature
Grand Staircase-Escalante National Monument

Mary Ellen Esposito   Children
Child's Delight

Gail M. Erickson   Children
The Thinker Of A New Generation

Charlene Ferguson   Children
Wow! wwwtoys.com

Sharon Swartwood   Nature
Sunset

Timothy Alowa   Other
Sanctuary For Birds

Brinda Dragoo   Children
My Grandson Dressed Up For Halloween—He Was A Girl

Laurie Weber   Children
Moving

Jim Ilsley   Children
Call To Santa

Mary Ann Hall   People
Indian Couple At Paye, AZ

Ruby R. Forrest   Animals/Pets
Pepper's Curiosity

Steven W. Ketterer   Other
Serenity

Lisa-Marie Mullen   Children
The Rolling Balls

Marie-Louise Buschinsky   Animals/Pets
Good Joke, Shared Between Friends

Greta Stanfill   Nature
Cumberland Falls

Brenda P. Ayscue   Nature
Plumeria, Flower Of Hawaii

Priscilla Charles   Animals/Pets
World's Best Partner

Dee O'Hara   Animals/Pets
Color

E. Clevenger   Travel
San Francisco Peaks, Near Flagstaff

Sharon King   Animals/Pets
Do Not Disturb

Sharilyn Deslauriers   Children
Catching The Falling Stars

Doris L. Saputo   Travel
Ancient Selinunte Ruins, Sicilia

Carrie Kuta   Animals/Pets
Best Friends

Marsha L. Watson   Nature
Daydreamer

Janet Brunory   Nature
Silent Night, Holy Night!

Rachel Coun   Other
Lock On Blue

Mary Salyers   Children
Bucket Of Love

Kim Triner   Other
Nathan And Bessie

Cheryl Feen   Children
You Can Leave Your Hat On

Julie Glasen   Other
Dusk On The Water

Donna Trepas   Nature
Crystal Morning

Kevin Silis   Nature
The Stare

Michael Eyler   Nature
Our Lady Of Mount Carmel

Jennifer Benigno   Animals/Pets
My Precious Buca

Deborah Schmidt   Animals/Pets
Ramses On His First Vacation

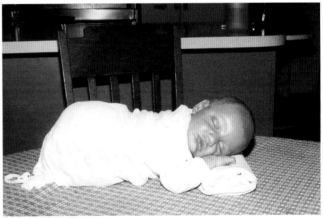

Kay Peabody   Children
When I'm Tired, I Can Sleep Anywhere

Carolee Stanfield   Animals/Pets
Bottle Time

Bonnie R. Combs   Animals/Pets
Fat Cat, Smoky

Marilyn J. Gentry
Waterfalls Out Of The Side Of The Mountain

Nature

George H. Brooks
Sunset Over Yellowstone Lake

Nature

Lorie Carr
The Beacon

Travel

Cherrol Anderson
Nature's Treat

Nature

Sue Leavitt
Winter's Soul Mate

Animals/Pets

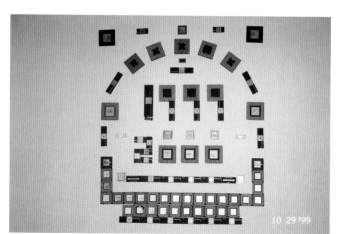

Mark Sandroni
Y2K

Other

Teresa M. Morgan Hosking Nature
Camping Trip On Our Way Up Pikes Peak In Colorado

Sherri Branson Animals/Pets
Simply Irresistable

Paul J. Wasklewicz Nature
A Spring Sunset

Anthony J. Bracha Children
Safe Drivers

Melinda Schwartz Travel
Castle Hill Light, Newport, RI

Joan Fornwalt Travel
No Ordinary Fence

Ethan Tilton　　　　　　　　　　Animals/Pets
Bonding

Alene Tincher　　　　　　　　　　Nature
Laural River In Corbin Kentucky

Anna Semones　　　　　　　　　　Other
The Lookout

Deeda Rhinehart　　　　　　　　　Portraiture
Contemplation

Jennifer C. Harris　　　　　　　　Animals/Pets
Out For The Count

Kris Meyer　　　　　　　　　　　Children
My Sunflower

Zerita J. Owen　　　　　　　　　People
Waiting

Mary G. Bennert　　　　　　　　Nature
Angry Skies In The Morning

Eileen Finlayson　　　　　　　Children
Discovering The Ocean

Nancy Zucco　　　　　　　Animals/Pets
Christmas Morning

Anita Wood　　　　　　　　　Nature
Beauty At Sea

Virginia L. Bouye　　　　　　Humor
Watch Your Tail, Sammy

Sandy McCool   Nature
Sedonda's Finest

Phyllis Sanderson   Children
Yellow Delicious Apples

Kathy Claybrook   Nature
Fly Like An Eagle

Carolyn Umphlett   Animals/Pets
Chance Waiting For Santa

Heather Cerankoski   Children
Granddaughter Autumn Cerankoski

Madean Ku   Children
Playing The Organ

Lirra Tolentino   Nature
Vermont, Fall 1999

Jackie Le Clair   Children
Copycat

Merle Dailey   Nature
Sunset

Matina L. Stamatakis   Nature
Rose

Toddi Frizzell   Nature
Evening's Eve

Vahagn Hovannesian   Animals/Pets
Kichwa Tembo Camp Monkey

Dianna Cavalieri   Other
Winter In Provincetown '99

Karen Babcock   Animals/Pets
It Was A Long Night

Jenny Agee   Children
Baby Green Eyes

Christopher Cogswell   Nature
Country Road

Melba R. Hizer   Animals/Pets
Yummy!

Heather Boccella   Children
Waiting For Poppy

Isabella White   Other
Pret-A-Porter For The Year 2001

Barbara Dabritz   Travel
Leeds Castle, Maidstone, Kent

Lisa Caughhorn   Nature
Breakfast

Patricia Rogers   Nature
Springtime

C. J. Kitchen   Nature
Babies Greet Each Other

Patricia Niebergall   Children
Mother Nature's Little Gardener

Don Dickinson Other
I Hope They Don't Get Any Bigger

Brian Carroll People
Best Buds

John Carlin Children
Friends Forever

Mike D. Williams Nature
Arizona Relaxation

Connie Gimbel Nature
Blazing Sunset

William A. Goodman Travel
The Hiding Light

Robert W. Hiltunen   Nature
Wachusett Old Stone Church

Angelo A. Grella   Children
Relaxing Music

Betty Garcia   Sports
Meeting The Ball

Nedra L. Bohrer   Animals/Pets
My Pomeranians—Fluff Kissing Angel

Lori K. Murphy   Children
Puppy Kisses

Teresa Ransom   Travel
A Pretty Sight

Jaki Handel
Pacific Sunset
Nature

Cindy Ardaiz
I Wanna Do That
Children

Lawanda Chain
Skyward Bound
Action

Robin Hatter-Taylor
Stoney And Friend
Animals/Pets

Edith Dale Edge
Best Friends
People

Kenneth James Taylor
Modern Reflections
Travel

Janet Goicoechea Animals/Pets
Can We Talk?

Greta Silverman Animals/Pets
Shall We Dance?

David Abuhl Nature
Sunset In Alaska

Glenda Burleigh People
Alone At The Bridge

Donna M. List Nature
Glorious Light

Janis S. Marsette Other
Silent Observer

Laura Miller   Nature
Buffalo

Doris R. Denyer   Action
Airborne

David Giordano   Children
Innocence

Jerry Tessmann   Nature
If Trees Could Talk

Larisa Johnson   Nature
Summer Blossoms

Eve World   Nature
Lily Pond

Judith A. Manson Children
Beach Blanket Beauty

Virginia M. Parks Travel
The Saturation Point

Bruce A. Holms Nature
Morning Mirror

Mary F. Miller Animals/Pets
Pretender

Cynthia Cross Nature
A Piece Of Maryland's Farmland

Veikko Huotari Other
Thief

Sam Judge Travel
Chariot By The Thames

Tammy Cunningham Portraiture
A New Beginning

Gene Hunt Nature
Pelican

Janene Bartos Animals/Pets
Polar Bear Play

Christine Haws Portraiture
Abandoned

Kathryn Dyer Czlapinski Action
The Tango Lesson

Sarajane White   Children
Hmm!

Cheryl Lee Kinney   Nature
Yosemite, God's Triumph

Vicki Powell   Nature
God's Bonus

Maria Sangirardi   Children
Beach Fun

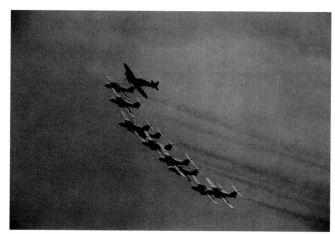

Richard Kunzmann   Action
Spitfire, Snowbird Fly By

Emery B. Tinley   Portraiture
Sitting Tall

Teri Wilson   Animals/Pets
Superman Cat

Martha Marcum   Children
October End

Donna Child   Nature
Tulips Divine

Stacey Banks   Children
Cowboy At Heart

Cathy Powers   People
Daddy's Little Girl

Shearline K. Baber   Children
Returning Home From First Day At School

Sarah Beth Tartaglia   Nature
Woodland Wonders

Gerald Vierra   Nature
Arizona Aspens

Gregory Itkin   Nature
Fall Colors In High Sierra California

Craig Rolander   Nature
South Arm Of Knife Lake

Lisa Lavergne   Children
Dawn Of A New Day

Heather Finnigan   Animals/Pets
Where'd Lunch Go?

Joanne Pillion Nature
Burst Of Light At Sunset

Mary Ann Rexrode Nature
Sunset In Winter

Carolyn Valentine Animals/Pets
What A Tale

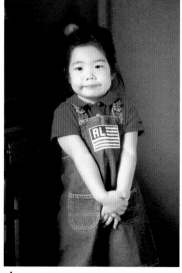

Atsushi Mikami Portraiture
Anna

Vera Kidwiler Animals/Pets
Purr-T-Flower

Dianna Cruz Nature
Lunchtime

Kathleen Bovo Children
Umbrella Fun

Lisa Whitney Animals/Pets
Cat Got Your Tail?

Deborah Hall-Tanksley Nature
Masterpiece By God

Jason C. Stigers Nature
Maroon Bells

Nadine Shadlock Children
Katharine's World

William A. Forsythe Animals/Pets
Roger Drives His School Bus

Denise Hurt Animals/Pets
I Have A Bone To Pick With You!

Anthony DelGrego Animals/Pets
Beginning Flight

Jennifer Choby Other
Sunrise At The Cross

Samuel Kling Children
Harvest Time

Esther Griffin Other
Can't Wait To Eat The Pear

Dolores Firth Travel
Hawaiian Sunrise

H. Prudence Nicholson
Water Art

Sports

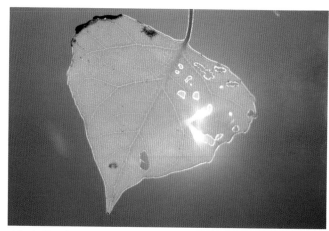

Alexis Berriman
November Shade

Nature

Raffaella C. Drummond
Angel Face

Children

Olga Herrera
Wow!

Children

Tami McGarvey Clark
I Love My Sister

Children

Judy Martenson
A Boy's Journey

Nature

Amanda Ralston   Nature
Solitude

Robert A. Leser   Children
What We Did Last Summer

James F. Davis   Nature
The Loch At Dusk

Linda D. Schurz   People
Hard Day At The Show

Daisy Suero   Nature
In The Garden

Joyce B. Correll   Humor
Sluggo Crunching

Joyce Counts Jones   Other
Fresh Seattle Seafood

Loa M. Schell   Nature
Dust Storm, Phoenix

Pam Lucas   Other
Train Bridge

Stephanie Cheng   Animals/Pets
Baby Mini

John A. Brawdy   Animals/Pets
Sheba's Birthday

Debra Kuffner   Nature
Shadow Fence

Addam Hatch   Humor
Stuck Out Tongue

Michael Hranac   Animals/Pets
Lester

Melissa L. Murphy   Animals/Pets
Want To Play?

Kenneth W. Nippert   Nature
Snatchaheelin

Kathy Keller   People
Urban Cowboy

Diana Locke   Nature
Lotus Odessy

Lorraine Barr   Children
Happiness To Share

Christopher Tuscan   Nature
Fall Here

Sharon Monroe   Children
Minnesota Autumn Nice

Daniel T. Squires   People
The Fuller Brush Man Having A Good Day

Kaye Miller   Travel
Ghost Town—Kolmanskop Namibia, Africa

Paul W. Madonia   People
Vietnam Memory

Cheryl C. Hall   Children
Halloween Bums, 1999

Alfred Emans   Nature
Marilyn's Poppies

Louise M. Kreuzer   Animals/Pets
No Worries, Mate

Beth Stakem   Children
I Love You Too

Carol Koenig   Animals/Pets
To Sleep, Willie Finds A Place

Lisa Kopchak   Animals/Pets
Mya

Melody Rosenberg   Travel
Looking Up To The Sears Tower!

Lauren Beitel   Nature
Home Free

Robert Jagar   Animals/Pets
Tennis Doubles

Denise Larsen   Nature
Stream Of Light

Alene S. Luffman   Nature
Sun At Myrtle Beach

Mildred E. Kellner   Children
Sooo Big!

Florence Mangione   Nature
Autumn Serenity

Catherine Louthian   Nature
Picture Perfect Fall

Laura Pittman   People
Bluebonnet Bride

Pegg Marmon-Ridolfo   Animals/Pets
Cool Down After A Tough Match

Ruth Waters   People
Buddy Sees Dad At Boot Camp

Katherine Marrone   Animals/Pets
I Am The Queen Of This House

Lori Q. Garcia   Children
Bumbleween

John M. Farney   Travel
Top Of Mt. Hood

Matthew W. Meyer   Children
Halloween Costume

John E. Hysom   People
Eternal Task

Deborah Olson   Children
The Prettiest Flower In The Garden!

Greg La Pres   Nature
Untitled

Pam Lantz   People
Dear Hearts Young And Old

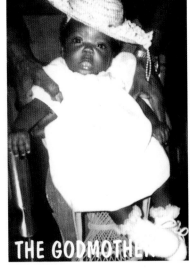

Alma Kirk   Humor
The Godmother

Elizabeth M. Braun   Animals/Pets
Essence

Nancy Ward   Children
The Count

Mary Ann Bonzi   Animals/Pets
Whittie—Nickname Blanco

Giovanna Concas   Children
No Spanking Thirty Feet Above

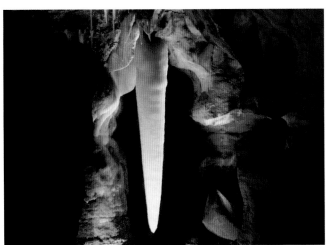

Connie Hudson   Nature
Hanging Tight

Lorrie Fitzgibbons   Children
Brotherly Love

Kim Wheeler   Other
Winter Wonderland

Linda Michael   Children
Sunshine Of My Life

Susan Price   Children
Cruisin'

Linda Sulpy   Nature
Endless Summer Sunset

Martha Hodges   Nature
Short And Tall Of People And Plants

Dorris Parker   Animals/Pets
Please, Don't Leave Me

Lana J. Lapp   Children
Jaimie And Friends

Carl M. Ackley   Animals/Pets
Wild Mallard Ducks On Hedges Lake

Remelle Adams   Nature
Reflection

Patricia Miller   Animals/Pets
Fall Fun

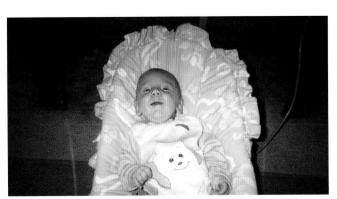

Lee Allen   Children
Personality Plus

Valeria Diaz   Humor
Mozart's Melody

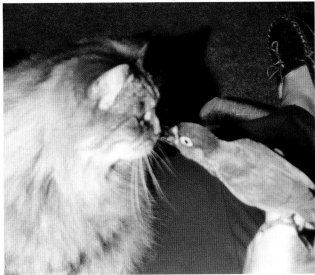

Robert Heath   Animals/Pets
Controlled And Supervised Visitation!

Todd Wood   Travel
Historic Reflections

Jennifer Blazkiewicz   Children
Bedtime

Eva M. Seifert   Children
Play Ball

Cindy Gregory   Nature
Sawtooth Up Close

Rebecca Lock   Nature
Serenity

Dorothy M. Strickland   Animals/Pets
Suzy's Ninth Birthday

Carl Clare   Animals/Pets
Now, Will You Quit Pestering Us For A Picture?

Carla Ford-Anderson   Animals/Pets
Okay, Okay, Merry Christmas Already

Patricia Pancake   People
Looking For Moose

Barbara D. Gaver   Humor
Down The Hatch!

Violet Greene   People
Bongainville In Full Bloom

Steven R. Back   Animals/Pets
Prarie Chicken Mating Dance

Tara Carroll   Children
Got Milk?

Barb O'Connell   Action
Riding The Waves

Mary A. Cornman   Nature
Caves On The Ocean

Heidi Menning   Children
Autumn In Wisconsin

Geneva Smith   Children
Bobbing For Apples

Jennifer Hoynoski   Children
The Girls

Valerie W. Young   Animals/Pets
Brotherly Love

Lindsay Bitzer   Nature
Beautiful Serenity

Sean Barry   Nature
Serenity

Ruth E. Kakacek   Nature
Mills And Steamboat Park

Anthony Graham   Nature
Blue Sky, Red Rock

Betty J. Smith   Animals/Pets
Snuggle Time

Patricia Gilson   Children
Me And Happy Dawg

Doreen Routledge   Other
Can We Be Friends?

Mary Raymond   Children
Trimin' The Tree And Me

Helle Martin   Children
Dayna Loves Rosco

Patsy Hogan   Children
Lesli And Che-Che

Rhea A. Dixon   Nature
Summer View

Lisa M. Ringer   Nature
Reflections On Mirror Lake

Imelda I. Serranilla   Nature
Here Comes The Greens

Charlene M. Kuznia   Nature
Dawn's Fresh Faces

Stella C. Card   Children
Up At Bat

Toni Beery   Children
Aden At The Lighthouse Door

Vivian Braubitz   Nature
Better Than Gold

Linda Mertens   Animals/Pets
Camoulflage Cat

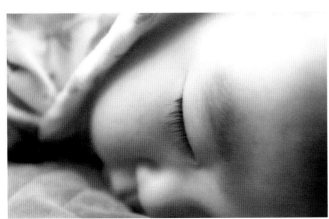

Chung H. Choe   Children
Peace

Linda Vandermer   Animals/Pets
Sassy

Echo Siakooles   Animals/Pets
A Flower Among Flowers

Linda Williams   Children
Big Smile!

Pat Larmoyeux   Humor
Puzzled In The Pumpkin Patch

Luciano Dos Santos   Nature
Fall

Roy Sullivan   People
Country Pose

Gregg Rupe   Nature
Sunrise At Myrtle Beach

Antone Starkey   Animals/Pets
White Hope

Ralph Cohen   Travel
View From Pier 66

Linda E. Reynolds   People
Early Morning Sun

Dennis Sears   Animals/Pets
Family Get-Together

John Murray   Animals/Pets
Kids At The Zoo

Sharon J. Slack   Travel
The Arch In An Arch

Gail McGregor   Nature
In The River At Chimney Rock

Genevieve Ayers   Children
Isn't There A Better Place To Lay?

Betty Underwood   Nature
The Gathering Clouds

Auran   Travel
Arlington In Autumn

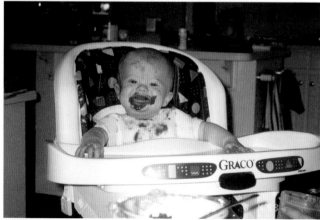

Merri Jo Pate   Children
Aahh! Delicious Blueberries

Tammy Cole   People
Never Give Up A Chance To Try!

Tiffany Payne Nature
Ice Storm

Louise M. Henson Children
Fascination With Skimmer Bags

Elizabeth Coughlin Other
A Boy And His Dog

Viola Irvin Children
Finding The Biggest!

Carla Sluga Children
A Day At The Beach

Tammy L. Holder Animals/Pets
Ready To Play

John Pelczar   Nature
The Beauty Of Sunset In Massachussetts

Audrey L. Sue   Nature
A Poinsetta Tree, A Holiday Speciality

Robert Patrick   Nature
Glowing Lilly

Jenny Walker   Nature
Be Still And Know

Christopher Sonnier   Nature
Tranquility

F. McCluskey   Action
Thunderbirds

Dianne Wood Animals/Pets
Buddies

Allison Andrews Animals/Pets
Peek-A-Boo

Wanda Carter Children
Making Memories

Alex White Humor
Boston In A Bean Patch

Diane Smith People
Ready For Take-Off

Katie Troha Children
Resting On The Tracks

Robin T. Wrench   Nature
Serenity

Jeanne P. Hamilton   Animals/Pets
Cookie Jar

Melissa Davis   People
A Day At The Fair

Jeffrey M. Emonds   Other
Stained View

Patricia Rardin   Children
Winning Shot

Joseph La Monica   Sports
Fighting For Control

Tom FitzSimon   Travel
A.M. Seascape

Sharon L. Kaczowka   Nature
Our Star

Cindy Pearson   Action
Shadows In The Wind!

Alice C. Bowman   Nature
A Mirrored Sunrise Over Daytona Beach

Judith Manley   Children
A Day In The Woods

K. Pulenthiran   Children
The Bliss

Danielle DelSontro   Children
Renee

Cheryl Bresch   Children
Courage

Carol Winkel   Children
Did You Say Ice Cream?

Vivian Barden   Nature
Potomac Sunrise

Ginny Basehore   Action
Silo Disappearing Into Fog During Soccer Game

Deborah Tanski   Children
Jessica And Her Stickers

Pauline Hinton Animals/Pets
Hunter In The Blooms

Donnette Zacca Children
Candy Collectors

Sherry Ashley Nature
Backdoor View

Pamela Atkinson Nature
Heavenly Gifts

Harry Petersen Animals/Pets
Precious Load

John Funk Children
I Said Bike, Not Bite

Leta Blevins Children
Jaime's Fourth Of July

Glynda Fawbush Animals/Pets
Cool Dude

David A. Werner Animals/Pets
I Didn't Get Picked

Edith Kelly Children
Ooh! What You Said

Barbara Buchholz Animals/Pets
Another Carrot Please!

Lynne Burns Animals/Pets
Let's Do Lunch

Barbara Dulman   Animals/Pets
Is My Collar On Straight?

Robyn A. Eggleston   Children
Splash!

Karen S. Hanna   Animals/Pets
Falling In Love

B. Faye Meadows   Nature
Kentucky Winter

Shirley J. Hudson   Nature
Oklahoma Heaven

Barbara J. Skidmore   Children
Only Been Kissed Once

Paula Valiton   Children
Like Father, Like Son

Jerry Haywood   Nature
God's Gift

Anita LaRico   Travel
Stonehenge

Judith Ogden   Animals/Pets
It Is Mine, Isn't It?

Tammy Curcio   Children
Gramma's Little Angel

Ida E. Nierman   Travel
And The Melody Lingers On

Margie Crawford   Nature
Sunset On The Sound

Jo Shuemaker   Nature
Sunrise At Wildwood Crest, NJ

Judy Reifenberger   Nature
Big Bird Watching Over Cornell Road

Paula A. DuRocher   Children
Taking Time To Stop And Smell The Flowers

Steven F. Hansen   Animals/Pets
Mmm, That Was Good

Jane Christensen   Animals/Pets
Mother And Son

Jeni Anderson   Children
Totally Speechless

Tracey Fowler   Portraiture
Me And My Best Buddy

Ann Ratanasavetavadhana   Nature
Straight Into The Andaman Sea

Sheryl Schuette   Animals/Pets
The Unsinkable Rijo

Cheryle Tillery   Humor
Key West Adventures

Janice Hedges   People
Bosom Buddies

Paul J. Haller   Nature
Sunset In The Smokies

Alison Miller   Animals/Pets
Please? Playtime For Summer?

Deanna Stawinski   Animals/Pets
Don't Touch! These Are All Mine

Karen Hoffman   Children
Glena And Sara Dancing

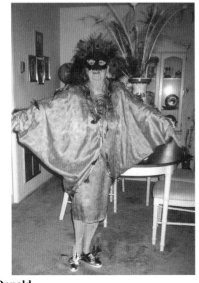

Leona McDonald   Humor
Grandma Peacock

Arlene J. Casey   Animals/Pets
Picture Of Patience

Jackie Pierce   Nature
Shadows

Olga Albertine   Animals/Pets
Daydreaming

Rosemary Jay   Nature
Serenity

Mary Fruth   Children
Eating Watermelon

Betty C. Crowell   Children
A Precious Moment

Robert Jessen   Children
Looking For A Big One

Cyneva Youngblood Animals/Pets
Her Majesty

Dustyn Noland Children
Shooting The Breeze

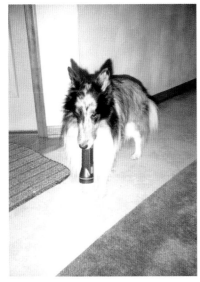

Fred Noel Animals/Pets
Watch Your Step

Ian Eric Cock Nature
A Floral Triumph

Brian Kuhn Travel
Mayflower Morning

Mandy Davis Children
You Can't See Me

Barbara Ellis   Children
Star Princess

Linda Fiore   Travel
Lost Luggage On A Cruise

John D. Long   Sports
Game-Winning Goal

Terry Clark   People
Cowboy Love

Kross Hamilton   Children
Just Like Tigger

Cindy Tirelli   Nature
Henrietta

Vincent LiVigni   Other
Death Of A Cabin

Edna L. May   Nature
Old Faithful In The Evening

Cordelia Hall   Animals/Pets
Sharing This Moment In Time

Linda M. Kasper   Animals/Pets
Bring On The Cold And Snow

Kim Sedillo   Children
Best Friends

Barbara Wheeler   Children
Contentment

Cindy Lea Lovejoy   Children
A Star Is Born

Terri Chivers   Nature
Autumn Path

Faye Gaston   Children
Pious Gratitude

Mary Sammartano   Animals/Pets
Balancing Act

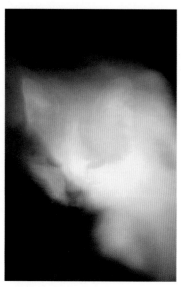

Robert Porch   Animals/Pets
Cat And Apparition

Willie Barber   Children
Caught, With Dirty Hands

Douglas L. Duell   Animals/Pets
Tired Out

Constance Bradley   Animals/Pets
Hurry Before I'll Drive Away And Leave You

Cindi Hanna   Nature
Looking Glass Falls

Linda Owens   Nature
Sunset Splendor

Sarah Rice   Children
Any Requests?

Betty J. Adams   Animals/Pets
Refuse Refuge

Neil R. Jeneral   Nature
Great Heron

Irene Linsky   Children
Life Is Beautiful

Brenda Johnson   Nature
Nature At Its Best

Mary Gewickey   Nature
Winter Spectacular

Gladys Chamberlain   Animals/Pets
Something As Sweet As Me

Leanne M. Dotson   Children
Lost In The Hay

Mitzi Miller   Children
Sweet Corn

Mary Roy   Children
My Little Pumpkin

Deb Dixon   People
What Can I Get Into Next?

Sarah Helderman   Children
Picking Wildflowers

Nathan D. Weller   Travel
Westminster's Glory

Donna Cope   Children
My Grandchildren

Sandra Ferguson Humor
Waterfalls' Beauty

Ellen Taylor Animals/Pets
Solitude In Autumn

Joan G. Stueber Children
Kid Talk

Charmion Franz Children
Friends Forever

Alicia McCullough Children
Elation

Jennifer W. Myers People
Mackenzie

Sandra Caslake   Nature
Animals

Deanne Morin   Animals/Pets
Trick And Treat

Baby Higuera   Animals/Pets
Baby In Tuna Can

Sally Rodenhiser   Animals/Pets
The Big Yawn

Anthony F. Afong   Travel
Keeping Watch

Judith Chisarik   Children
Emily

Eleanor Baribault   Animals/Pets
Image Of Me

Mary Duncan   Animals/Pets
Why Pay Salon High Prices, When You Can Do It Yourself

Irvin Williams   Travel
Hotshot In Japan

Ronald Jackson   Humor
Best Cookies In The World

Grace Marines   Nature
Western Sunset

Larisa Kulikova-Bray   Children
My Russian Son In Vietnam, 1992

Nikki Lenhart   Humor
Action Wheelbarrow By My Father-In-Law

Nancy S. Ward   Nature
The Cloudy Day

Lula M. Hooks   Animals/Pets
Sneaking A Nap With My Husband

Joel K. Blatchford   People
Living In The Boonies

Janet Harris   Travel
God's Awesome Beauty

Charles Anthony   Nature
First Snow At Old Laveta Pass In Colorado

Marty A. Harriman   Children
Buckaroo Blues

Vicki Frazee   People
Halftime On The Soccer Field

Laura H. Darsey   Nature
Blooming Hibiscus

Mary Scheinberg   Children
Did He Really Say My Name?

Helen L. Bradley   Nature
Autumn Early Morn

Barbara Parrett   Animals/Pets
Here We Go Again?

Karen Carroll   People
Isn't She Beautiful?

Collins Gibson   Nature
Sunbathing

Juan C. Manzanares   Animals/Pets
What's Our Flight Number?

Judy Robinson   Children
Friends Forever

Sylvia Lock   People
Untitled

June T. Higdon   Nature
Autumn Sunrise

Karen Runk Children
Take Time To Smell The Pumpkins

Kim Vail Nature
Anything Is Possible

Joyce Braithwaite Nature
Sunset Spectacular

Jennie C. Rhodes Nature
The Power And The Glory

Geri Scheckler Nature
Hummers

Kristina DeMarco Nature
Regeneration

Denise Amburgey   Other
Smith Mountain, VA

Daren S. Davis   Children
Having Fun

Frank Anthony Cara   Humor
Two Scoops To Go Please!

Betty L. Cummings   People
Love Is Ageless

Philip S. Renaud   Animals/Pets
The Reader

Christine Bates   Travel
Cow's Eye View

Ray Schell Children
Please . . . Can I Have Some More?

Arlene Ham Nature
Serenity

Ron Evans People
Mother's Day '99, Mom Gets A Break!

Betty Lofland Children
Little Cowgirl

Florine M. Mahoney Travel
Bermuda Beach

Vera Life Nature
Two Squirrels Holding Nuts On Both Sides Of The Tree

Kelly Roberts   Nature
Storm On The Sea

L. G. Espinosa   People
Wedding Bride

William E. Mullikin   Animals/Pets
The Loving Rott

Sharon Michaux   People
The End Of The Day

Colleen Franchuk   Children
Smelling Wowers

Juanita Lainhart   Children
Papa's Little Man

Tammy Pritchard   Animals/Pets
The Boss Has Arrived

Carolyn Launchbury   Travel
Mediterranean Dawn, November 10

Diane Reppucci   Animals/Pets
What A Day

Kathy Greig   Nature
Well, Hello

Karen O'Connor   Children
Pumpkin Anyone?

Elba Cruz Pellot   Humor
Ugg! Daddy Smell, Real Bad

Helen E. Hornick Nature
The River Of Life

Jamie Kathleen Rodgers Animals/Pets
Bobby

Natalia Pevec Animals/Pets
Cold Canadian Winter To Come

Lawanda R. Harrington Nature
Niagara Falls

Denise Amick Nature
Serenity

Stephanie Markert Animals/Pets
Dog Gone Day

Marcella Bogan   Children
First Lesson—I'm Ready!

Ellen Witzel   Children
I'm A Doll Too

Clara Scott   Animals/Pets
Pointing Guard Rockey

Gladys Pardee   Nature
Winter's Beauty

Heather Helbach-Olds   Animals/Pets
Sady And Soup

Marlene Cusano   People
Guardian Angel

Katherine Akers   Animals/Pets
Grateful Kiss

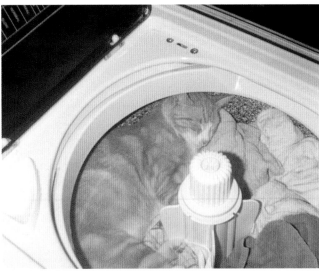

Michelle Adams   Animals/Pets
Ringgold's Bath

Jerry O. Fleming   Nature
Fall In The Sierras

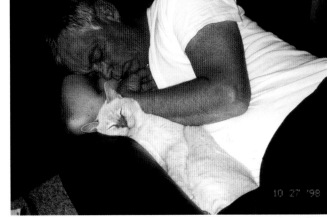

Beth Wilson   Animals/Pets
Cat Nap

Paula Schwertner   Animals/Pets
Emma Sitting Prettty

Stella Stamos   Animals/Pets
Stop And Smell The Flowers

Chris Penner   Animals/Pets
Quiet, I'm Watching Television

Joseph E. Gibbons   Animals/Pets
Panda Bear

Cassandra Moss   Children
My Precious New Baby Sister

Mary L. Geierman   Animals/Pets
Peek-A-Boo

Ginger Maune   Children
Don't Mess With Me

Clara Belle Gibson   Animals/Pets
Five Pounds Of Terror

Betty Meek   Children
Holly

Brian K. Talley   Nature
Elohim, God Our Creator

Sheila L. Fulton   Animals/Pets
My Bodyguard

Ellen Hefner   Children
Being Inconspicuous

Theresa M. Barnes   Children
Starting Young

Debbie Sallet   Children
Waiting For Daddy

Ailsa Faye Sundy   Travel
Southern Church

Ann Free   Animals/Pets
Tammy's Bed

Almira Wall   Nature
Mountain Lion

Michelle De Pietro   Animals/Pets
Tammy, Buffy, And Bambi—Doggie Kisses

Rita M. Matozzo   Children
The Amazing Tony

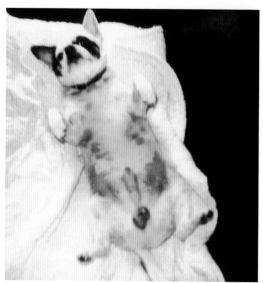

Barbra Steckter   Animals/Pets
Spike

Julie La Reau Travel
A Distant Light

Drew Wales Children
Danielle

Jackie Pignataro Sports
Game Face

Linda Grzeskowicz Animals/Pets
Phoebe

Russ Olson Nature
Canyon Clouds

Leonard F. Carol Animals/Pets
Let's Talk

Jeremy Lazzara　　　　　　　　　　Travel
Liberty At Sunset

Valerie Zasadny　　　　　　　　　　Nature
Sharing Lunch

Mary Ehrlinger　　　　　　　　　　Children
The Birthday Wish

Albert Stepnoski　　　　　　　　　　Nature
Comet Hale-Bopp

Larry Deyoung　　　　　　　　　　Nature
Owl

Faye A. Kennedy　　　　　　　　　　Children
Trying On Mom's Wedding Veil

Martha S. Kozak   Other
Extinction

Carolyn Caudill   Animals/Pets
Dalton And Cowboy, Friends

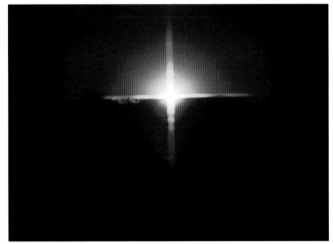

Art Merrihew   Nature
Evening Sunset

Niles Peasley   Nature
Broken But Beautiful Butterfly

Larry Nowakowski   Animals/Pets
I'm So Tired

Anne Petherbridge   Portraiture
A Watchful Eye

Kari Ried   Nature
Waterfall

John Bettfreund   Animals/Pets
Move Over

Scott Dzimian   Nature
Morning Dew On Spider Web

Pauline Renaud   Travel
Canterbury, Portal In Time

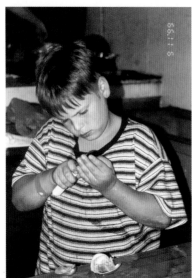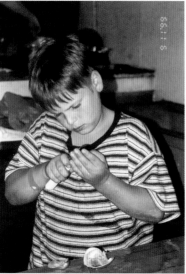

Brandon Ortiz   Children
Oyster Boy

Bob Adams   People
Sexy On The Beach

Francine McGraw   Nature
Winter Blues

Mary Cook   Other
Solitude

Marie Armstrong   Nature
Arches Of Nature

Tammy Retherford   Children
The Melon Man's Little Princess

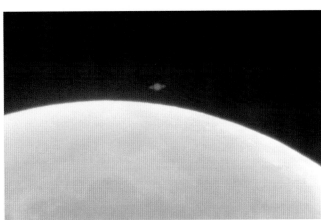

Victor Rogus   Nature
Our Moon And Saturn In Close Conjunction Before Occultation

Burnadean Winnell   Animals/Pets
White Beagle

Debbie Dutro   Travel
Eiffel Tower

Katie Myrmel   People
Bianca

John Emanuelli   Travel
Alaska Reverie

Judith H. Adkins   Children
Hard Day!

Nora J. Virrey   Portraiture
Young Boy

Judy Johnson   Children
Oh, Fresh Air

Karen Haffenbredl Animals/Pets
I'm Too Sexy For My Shirt

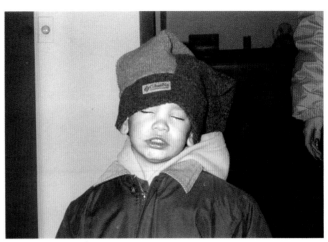

Marsha Neuschwanter Children
The Little Dreamer

Andrea Giovonizzi Animals/Pets
Happy Halloween

Joyce Miranda Other
Bahama Dusk

Willis Pierre People
Brotherly Admiration

Eva Wilkinson People
Age Makes No Difference To Friends

Carolyn Tracy   Children
My Little Angel

DeLane Nyberg   Animals/Pets
Sand In My Face

Bobbie J. Pope   Nature
Fog In The Smokies

Verna G. Heisler   Animals/Pets
Lazy Natasha

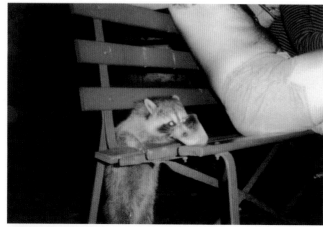

Robert Ziemba   Animals/Pets
One For The Road

Dan Hopkins   Animals/Pets
The Lookout

Reta L. Zody   Children
Todd And Starla

Diane Hyre   Nature
A Peaceful Mountaintop

Sheryl Padjen   Nature
Safe Refuge

Alicia Skipper   Animals/Pets
Dog Waiting

Julia Cronin   People
Holly

Denise Williams   Children
Morning Cartoons!

Vince Scapellato   Nature
Fenwick Sunrise

Seth Shimkonis   Other
Reflection Wheel

Jan Bargeron   Children
I Love You Prissy

Sondae Bosnak   Other
On The Verge Of Flight

Mathilda George   Children
Meditation

Megan Church   People
A Sense Of Disgrace

Bernard J. Bazydola   People
Babusia

Joanne Masher   Nature
Serenity

Wm. Charlesworth Jr.   Children
Andrew

Susan Evans   Nature
Zion

Barbara Orlando   Children
Pensive

Ben Lorentz   Other
Dusk Over Cowtown

Mary Ann Kulp   Animals/Pets
Reaching Higher Goals

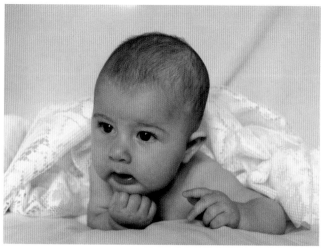

Maureen Greene   Children
Bella Rose

Edward M. Jackoboice   Nature
Iguazu Falls, South America

Merrilee Pedigeau   Animals/Pets
Wanna Play?

Colleen Roberta Diltz   Animals/Pets
Turtle Under Water

Jan Clayton   Nature
Storm Over Colorado Springs, CO

Beth Zemel   Nature
Seeing From The Dark

Rebecca M. Huston   Children
My Little Fishie

Garland L. Wood   Animals/Pets
Twins, Coty And Ginger

Cailin Anderson   Animals/Pets
Daily Prayers

Shawn L. Call   Children
The Watering Hole

Elise R. Mills   Animals/Pets
Peek-A-Boo!

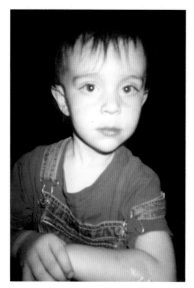

Minnie Evans   Children
I Have An Ouchie

Ginger Dugas   Animals/Pets
Yum!

Randy Sloan   Nature
Peaceful Autumn Morning

Lynne Schmidt   Animals/Pets
I'd Rather Be Walking

Kathy Knapczyk   Animals/Pets
Miracle Puppy Sleeps

Yu-Ting Chang   Animals/Pets
Meow-Ar

Thomas Piscitello   Animals/Pets
Stella Couture

Wilma Cook   Nature
Majestic Moment

Ellen Berris   Animals/Pets
Birthday Girls

Debi Callahan   Children
Move Over, Rover

Trudy Vincent   Nature
Working Spider

Diana McCallister   Children
Jason, Jeremy, And The Balloon

Diane Lawendowski   Animals/Pets
No End In Sight

Judith Rudderham   Nature
Pathway To The Sea

Kenneth Beerman   Nature
Butterflies In Full Bloom

Cindy Ehrhardt   Animals/Pets
You Don't Think You're Leaving Without Me, Do You?

Ralph De Vico   Animals/Pets
Protector Of The Garden

Amber Kiwan   Animals/Pets
Tuckered

Barbie Koncher   Animals/Pets
Here Comes Winter

John Mohr   Nature
Sunrise

Renee Weiss   Animals/Pets
Copy Cat

Janeen Lake   Travel
Passage Through Land's End

Julie Padrnos   Nature
Nesting Kill Deer

Susan Stolberg   People
Street Corner No. 12

Helen E. Drake   Nature
Irrigation's Icicles

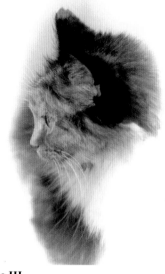

George C. Disse III   Animals/Pets
Snickers

Charlie Farrell   Animals/Pets
Tiger In The Garden

Devin Aumend   Nature
Bird Of Prey

Mark Deutsch   Other
Mark's Sneakers

Melissa Campbell   Nature
Fans

Andrew Stasieczek — Animals/Pets
The Time Of Feeding

Marguerite Novicke — Children
Bobby And Stripe

Stephen Hardesty — Nature
City Waterfowl

Charles M. Caizzi — Other
Kaboom!

Charlene Demello — Children
Freedom

Bonnie J. Meyer — Other
Great Game

Chauncy Smardon   Other
Ice Storm

Jewell Kellett   Animals/Pets
North Carolina Hummingbird?

Linda Alloway   Animals/Pets
Upside-Down Day

Carolyn Dalton   Portraiture
Contemplating The Wonders Of Life

Karen Leshkivich   Animals/Pets
Gibson

Katie Abbott   Children
Happiness

Nancy K. Sanders   Other
Americana At Its Best

Cassie Bowles   Nature
Fall Beauty

Joe J. Messina   Animals/Pets
Relaxing Rabbit

Susanne Marzani   Children
You Need A What To Drive?

Sonja Wright   Animals/Pets
Little Man On His Throne

Zydre Obrikiene   Children
Rest

Kathy Faulkner-Youngren   Animals/Pets
The Grape Sphinx

Jeton Karahoda   Other
Broken Dreams

Kathleen Revell   Animals/Pets
Must You Use Me As A Chair?

Tony Higgins   Children
Fall Innocents

Ruth Ann Myers   Animals/Pets
Joined At The Head

Waltraud A. Milani   Animals/Pets
Doggy In The Shadows

Henry Stockhausen   Children
Leyna, Our Princess

Ralph L. Slayman   Nature
Soft Surf

Misti Pattison   Children
Nate The Great At The Quarry

Charlotte A. Stiver   Animals/Pets
I Told You, My Name Is Mary D. Lou!

Edwin W. Howald   Nature
Outdoor Gourmet

Alicia R. Drew   Children
Time Out For Two

Dianne Hickman Nature
Heaven's Reflection

Tina Ray People
Grandma's Eightieth Birthday

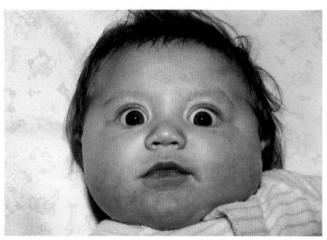

Laura Harris Children
The Eyes Have It

Mary Green Nature
Oregon Sunset

Linda L. Behrendt Nature
Coast Of Maine

Ruth D. Johnson Nature
Maro Lake, Goose Island, Glacier National Park

Ann McNally Travel
Reflections

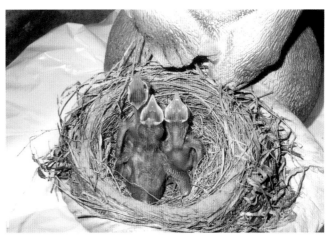

Pat Greloch Nature
Where's Dinner?

Domenick Fanelli Travel
Chapel On The Mountain

Kalona Kierstede Children
Comfort

Elizabeth Giordano Nature
Untitled

Jack Adams Animals/Pets
Lonely Dog

Mindy McCutchan   Nature
Sugar Creek

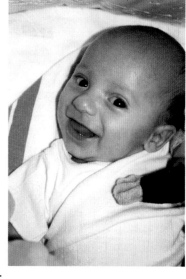

Steven Sitter   Children
Mr. Happy-Go-Lucky

Patricia L. Lehman   Children
The Sneaker

Walter Meisner   Nature
A Portal Into Nature

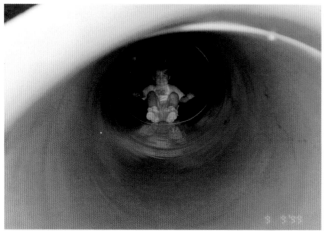

Lois Howat   Children
Peyton's Great Adventure

Marlene Hintz   Children
Mud Mania

Richard Lipinski   Animals/Pets
Sleeping Beauty

Jessica Coe   Nature
Reflecting Clouds

Kathleen McDonald   Children
The Awesome Ocean

Andrew A. Spalding   Nature
Fiery Morning

Claudia Anderson   Nature
Sunset Silhouette

Megan Reilly   Nature
Good Morning, Alaska

Tiemchan Changachit   Humor
One For Dinner

Jean H. Wonser   Children
Go For The Carrot

Jena Scott   Children
Emma

Mark K. Shaw   Nature
Dancin' Dolphins

Civita Orgera   Nature
Night Beauty

Barbara Dalton   Children
Rainy Day Fun

Carole Flott Animals/Pets
Gracie By The Verbena

Zhihua Sui Animals/Pets
Perfect Listener

Louis Heffron Animals/Pets
Stop And Smell The Roses

Cindy Belaus Animals/Pets
Lounging In The Afternoon

Janet S. Cruikshank Animals/Pets
Mmmm, Good!

Sandra Lorenz Animals/Pets
Old Dog Days Of Summer

Mary Kiskinen   Nature
Pots Of Gold

Danielle Hamaker   Animals/Pets
Marilyn Monroe, Move Over

Vanessa Quate   People
Man Of God

Paula Bratz   Children
Green-Eyed Angel

Myron M. Miller   Nature
Late November Visitor

Tyler Louis Albers   Children
Trick Or Treat

Michelle Seibert   Nature
Colors In the Badlands

Poppy Johnson   Humor
Leaf-It-To Floyd

Virginia Puckett   Children
Caught In The Act

Mark Jones   Portraiture
Summertime

Mark W. Watkins   Children
How Do I Look?

Ann W. Billings   Animals/Pets
Perfect Peepers

Natalia Del Rosario
Images Of Yesterday

People

Kenneth J. Russ
Illusions

Other

Chris McIntyre
Land Of Enchantment

Travel

Mary Ann Cavalieri-Burns
I Want To Go Home

Humor

Blake Robinson
Rainy Day Special

Children

Jim Jancaitis
Escape

Animals/Pets

Judy Franze   Nature
Tower Falls

Jean Houck   Nature
The Lane To Home

Catherine Lord   Travel
View From A Covered Bridge

Brett Passarella   Nature
American Fences

Roseann M. Noble   Nature
Christ, In The Clouds

Theresa Ann Giaimo   Animals/Pets
Her First Pacifier

Marianne Stratikopoulou   Nature
Untitled

Debby Losurdo   Travel
Florida Sunrise

Nancy Benson   People
Until Tomorrow

J. John Madia   Travel
On The Road

Lisa M. Nielsen   Nature
Serenity

Jackie Heryford   People
Fishing Buddies

William Amann　　　　　　　　　　　　People
Kremlin Mimicry

Gabrielle Boerkircher　　　　　　　Animals/Pets
Hidden Treasure

Paula Lyn Farmer　　　　　　　　　Children
Beach Baby

Justin Blower　　　　　　　　　　　Animals/Pets
Lizzard Tales

Debbie L. Anderson　　　　　　　　Animals/Pets
Nap Time

Richard Scheels　　　　　　　　　　Children
Sleeping Beauty

Valerie Chevalier   Children
Little Pumpkins

Susan Bunner   Other
Reflections

Kenneth Dech   Animals/Pets
Wild Friends

Kelly L. Cochran   Travel
Memories That Last A Lifetime

Larry Clark   Nature
After The Storm

Jill Schlefstein   Children
Time Out

Michael James Coon   Animals/Pets
Cute As Could Be

Luciana Geyer   Nature
Double Rainbow Over Miller Lake

Nancy E. Payne   Nature
Bobcock State Park, WV

Ed Stickles   Nature
God's Creation

Jim Coffey   Nature
Dripping Springs

Martha C. Hutchinson   Animals/Pets
Kitty Is Thirsty

Melissa Todd   Children
Sing

Adlah Donastorg   Nature
Cool Runnings

Jadd Awad   Children
Chilling Out

Alfha E. Parra   Action
The Drop Zone

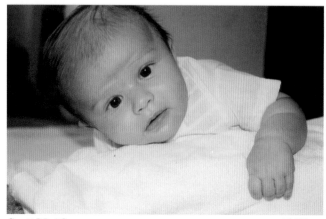

Scott McAfee   Children
Brown-Eyed Boy

Heather Robinson   Children
I Am Cutie Doll

Ricardo Ruiz   Other
The Bells Of San Juan Capistrano

Wyatt Irwin   Children
Wyatt Irwin—Ready To Go Farming

Amy M. Barkman   Animals/Pets
The Boys

Ruth Puffett   Animals/Pets
Waltzing Across Missouri

Harold Sims   Animals/Pets
Flower Child

William R. Love   Animals/Pets
Misty

Johnita Ferguson   Children
Cheyenne Harvest

Carol Heisler   Children
Sweet Lydia

Andrea Alexander   Nature
Anna Ruby Falls, GA

Carmen L. Maldonado   Nature
Tecaumena Fall Bay

M. L. Hyatt   People
Family Surprise

Coleen Zylka   Children
Basketful Of Joy

Margaret Harbour   Nature
Fall Reflections

Katherine Bursese   Other
Carly

Andrew Golovanov   Nature
Waterfall In Watkins Glen

Dottie Cowan   Nature
Dusk's Delight

Cathi Carpenter   Children
Audrey

Lucille Kam   Children
Mom, Is There Anything In My Eyes?

Rita McCarter   Children
Summer Vacation

James Holzinger   Other
Day's End

Geaneen Archer   Children
Marine Prodigy

Wilma Lemos   Travel
Siesta On The Beach

Britta McNish   Children
Savannah Smiles

May Duchene   Other
Untitled

Darla Infield   Nature
Summer Skies

Mara Toledano   Animals/Pets
Reflections Of The Beach

Joanne Kirschenbaum   Other
My Buddy And Me

Doris J. Olsen   Children
Peek-A-Boo

Paul Wagner   Animals/Pets
What, Me!

Nichoal Santa   Animals/Pets
Majestic Serenity

Mary Oberlin   Nature
Sunrise In Myrtle Beach

Larry D. Leiman   Children
Anticipation

Steven D. Cohen   People
Hawaii Wedding

Ramona Cruz   Nature
Beauty

Charles E. Wilhelm   Travel
The Coliseum

Nancy Schollhammer   Children
God's Gift

Cindy Holmberg Action
Brian At The Family Pool Party

Andrew A. Callahan Nature
Sunset

Christine Fink Children
Angel In The Garden

Suzette M. Adam Animals/Pets
Nature's Wonders

Soren Nielsen Animals/Pets
Beauty Of Nature

Salli Kowalski Animals/Pets
Playtime

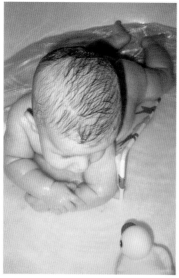

Melissa Kern   Children
The Wonder Of A Child

Sandra Shipton   Children
Is This All There Is To Life?

Laura Beardsley   Animals/Pets
Devil Dog

C. L. Colten   Nature
Minnesota Fall

Barbara A. Weber   Children
Havin' A Ball

Argentina A. Damian   Travel
The Way To Go

Kelly L. Chase People
Teachers Of Teachers Are We

Sherry McTeer Wright People
Bay Area Bonds Blast

Sharon Ann Raab Animals/Pets
Just Another Pretty Face

Kathleen Murphy Nature
Peaceful Moment

Mike Bertasso Animals/Pets
The Friendly Pig

Karla Badacour Humor
Playing With Dad

Judith Binger   Animals/Pets
Playtime

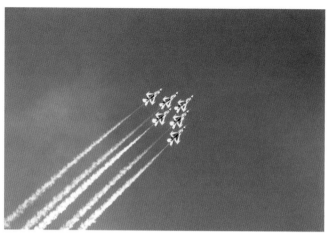

Michael Williams   Action
Thunder Birds Air Show

Amber Russell   Nature
Majestic Mountains

Marilyn Arnold   Children
Sisterly Love

Sherri L. Hamilton   Animals/Pets
Wanna Play?

Sharon Hall   Children
Nature's Beauty

Barbara Justice Nature
Vacation, October 1999

Viola Levito Nature
Solitude

Anthony De Rosa Travel
Conch Sailing Boat

June Jones People
Captured Aura

Debra Scheiding Animals/Pets
Puppy Love

Kasch McInnis Children
My Brother Masen

J. F. Pusch   Nature
Sunrise Over Crex Meadows

Shelley R. Loewnau   Nature
Green Lizard King

Sofia Gallina   Animals/Pets
Pigsty Snooze

Ron Russo   Travel
Surf Sound Set

Rebecca Potter   Children
My First Halloween

J. C. Porter   Children
Electrifying Swing

Shirley L. Hendrickson   Animals/Pets
I'm Just Adding To The Water!

Margaret Normile   Nature
A Tranquil Sunset

Lily G. Gunderson   Animals/Pets
So Exhausted

Vernon L. Sauder   Children
Cute Smooch

Daniel Nedeau   Travel
Fairbanks, Mountains, Alaskan Cruise 1999

Gabriella Nagy   Nature
Under The Tree

Angelina Askoak   Nature
God's Golden Creation

Brian Evrett   Nature
Mother's Love

Kitty M. Izor   Animals/Pets
Friends

Robert Sherman   Children
I Should Have Taken Ballet Instead

Walter Waggaman   Nature
Autumn On The Lake

Shirley H. Miller   Nature
Tree On Fire

Heidi DeCourcey   Children
Andrew's Pumpkin

Mary E. S. Cartwright   Children
My Water Baby

Kathy Wehnes   Nature
Yellowstone At Dusk

June Palivoda   Other
Sharing With A Friend

Deborah Johnson   Animals/Pets
Bonnie Sticking Her Tongue Out

Jearldine Clack   Animals/Pets
Baby Monique

Terri A. Hansen Children

Friends

Debra Benjamin Animals/Pets

Skunk Leaves Through Cat Door After A Snack On Cat Food

James R. O'Donnell Travel

O-K Bridge

Gary L. Steinbach Nature

In The Autumn Of The Day

Marian Fosdal Travel

Young Bather At The Amazon River

Elizabeth Cummins People

Daddy's Little Girl

Janice Geraw   Humor
I Love Vermont

Hunter Helin   Animals/Pets
Lunchtime

Barbara A. Wright   Nature
Snowfall's Serenity

Sally Flores   Animals/Pets
Ain't Life Grand

Kathryn Warne   Animals/Pets
Best Friends

Karen Rampone   People
Don't Look Back

Patti Boesgaard   Travel
Autumn In Vermont

Forrest R. Rader   Nature
Early Morn Snow

Mary Krull   Animals/Pets
Best Friends

Lisa Trapold   Nature
Serenity

Cherry L. Toland   Animals/Pets
Bear Necessities

Carley Kaba   Children
Ain't Love Grand

Oscar Cueto   Other
A New Beginning

Lou Ellen Klints   Animals/Pets
Blackie Makes Ripples

Paul Ruley   Travel
Montana Barn

Lloyd Holmes   Nature
Last Reflections Of 1999

Janice Dutton   Children
Concentration

Hilde Erenyi   Children
Pit Stop

Dave Chen   Nature
A Secret Among Friends

Jewell Riggin   Nature
Sitting Pretty

Glenn E. Stoner   Nature
Chuska Mountains

Jennifer Parker   Nature
Life's A Birch

Catherine Schoenherr   Children
First Fishing Trip

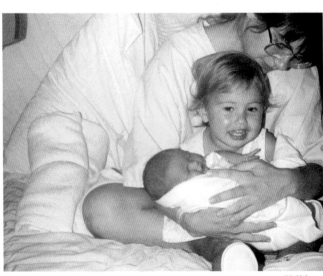

Sara E. Morales   Children
Love

Beulah Lacaillade   Nature
Rainbows On A Summer's Eve

Mary Cundiff   Children
What's Going On In There With That Turkey?

Karen L. Phillips   Animals/Pets
Serenity

Marilyn Allen   Nature
Spring Beauty

Alva P. Smith   Animals/Pets
Pig Being Bottle-Fed

Jacquie Hoekstra   Nature
Morning Frost

Valerie Hodge   Animals/Pets
Cadbury Puppy

Melissa Morin   Nature
Rocky Shore

Bessie A. Bowers   Nature
Let Your Imagination Soar

Erik Deste   Nature
West Side, South Beach Crescent City, CA

Jennifer Freeman   Animals/Pets
Bathing In The Sun

Lawrie Butler   Travel
Farewell Moorea, French Polynesia

Eleanor Moore   Travel
Calanais Stones

Sylvia M. Dollhopf   Children
Sweet Innocence

Beth Abrams   Nature
Sunset

L. D. Rice   Children
Joy

Rose Mary E. Marriott   Animals/Pets
Pretty Bird

Diana Lammermeier   Children
Caught Red-Handed

Jack A. Norwood　　　　　　　　　　　Animals/Pets
Peek-A-Boo

Laurel Horton　　　　　　　　　　　People
Friends In Nature

Bonita Hanshaw　　　　　　　　　　　Nature
Just A Little Spat

Charles Bursiel　　　　　　　　　　　Nature
Light And Shadow

Randy Dye　　　　　　　　　　　Nature
Tranquility

Agustin A. Leyva　　　　　　　　　　　People
Eyes Of Innocence

Lynn Farrell Animals/Pets
We Look Up To You

Glenda Smith Nature
Frosty Morning Surprise

Jean-Claude Macrez Travel
Bosilic And Venice

Elaine Arthur Children
Bubble Bath

Melissa Jackson Other
Reverie

Audrey Silva Nature
Texas Skies

Debora Peda   Children
Pumpkin Patch

Gay Monroe   Animals/Pets
Little Cat

Paul Saltenberger   Nature
Up And Away

Angie J. Tolman   Nature
Hidden Beauty

Karin Peiler   Animals/Pets
Getting To Know Each Other

JulieAnn R. Rahkola   Animals/Pets
Did You Get All The Fleas?

Les Smith Nature
Masterpiece Of Nature

Iliana Ramos Carrol Animals/Pets
Taking An Afternoon Stroll

Barbara Brady Animals/Pets
Lunch

Ron Bach Children
What A Boat Ride, Grandpa

Ed Stuhmer People
A Step Back In Time

Kimberly Coon Children
Ice Cream Lover!

Cathy Draxler   Nature
A Cooling Splash!

Roxanne Brydges   Animals/Pets
Right Of Way

Michelle Alfaro   People
Baby-Watching

Brian W. Kaatze   Animals/Pets
White Horse

Michael Lee Wills   Other
Opioid

Doug Davidson   Animals/Pets
When Turkeys Attack

Mark A. Brown   Nature
Towering Moon

Gerri Duke   Nature
Nature's Contrasts

Kathy J. Kiplinger   Nature
Colors Of Heaven

Robert Hopkins   Nature
Laura's Wood

Curtis A. Gibbens   Nature
The Tail Of A Whale

Charles T. Riley   Nature
Mountain Serenity

Dennis E. Smith   Nature
The Flight To Success

Barbara May   Nature
Solitude

Virginia Brigance   Children
Just One More Bite Please

Terry Rowe   Animals/Pets
Pendamai With Mom, Jill

Marilynn Stiger   Nature
Spiderweb

Judith E. Breckenridge   Children
Morro Bay

Kelly Grace Eaddy Portraiture
The Ravage Of Time

B. Johnson Other
Sunset On Harbor

V. T. Ildefonso Children
Halloween Doggie

Don McCray Animals/Pets
We Can't All Be Beauty Queens!

Edmundo Molina Travel
Mystic Paradise

Kenneth And Fetta Moore Nature
Dunes In The Fall

Kim W. Smith   Nature
Quiet Reflection

Kimberly M. Tutera   People
Innocent Curiosity

Thien Tang   People
Feel Smug

Jean F. Russo   Children
My Scarecrow

Susan Beiersdorff   Nature
Wisconsin Sunset

Patricia Sowinski   Children
I'm Confused, Mom's Starting Over

Richard Kenna   Animals/Pets
Cozmo

Sarah Steele   Other
It's Been A Long Life

Howard Harrison   Other
In The Moment

Susie Kiemschies   Nature
Footprints

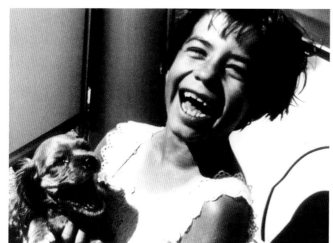

Marcelino Martinez   Children
My Best Friend Keeps Me Laughing

Sheron Davis   Nature
Cattails In Spring

Paul Marra Nature
Going For Take-Out

Irene Macmillan Animals/Pets
Alpine Fun

Joseph J. Neff Nature
Mother's Love

Lidonna Wallat Animals/Pets
White Peacock

Rollin B. Child Nature
Proud Parents

Milt Danoff Travel
Hanging Out!

Frank Steiner Humor
Bodies Do Not Last

Luis Alvarez Travel
Night Burn

Dale Teubert Nature
Sierra Buttes Lookout After A Spring Storm

Douglas R. Campbell Nature
Rising To The Occasion

Ivan Halksworth Nature
Sunset, Swan Range

Kenny Vuong People
After Harvest Season

Sherrie H. Sinclair   Animals/Pets
A Dog's Life In Paris

Virginia Gail Mobley   Nature
Awesome Wonder

Terry Fain   Travel
Kenai Lake

Marianne Nardandrea   Nature
Gator In The Clouds

Sissie Young   Nature
Arizona Cowboy Birder

Rita A. Erney   Nature
Reflection

Jennifer Anderson People
Home

Daniel Shepardson Travel
Hindu Sentinels

Hung Nguyen People
Untitled

H. Francis Whiting Other
New Hampshire Schoolhouse

Marie Kadisha Davidson Children
Watch Out

Jacqueline Killilea Nature
Just Curious

Ginger Gaskell Children
Christmas Angel

Dorothy Pankratz Action
Pitching In

Betty Crocker Nature
Graceful Reflections

Michael Robert Asbury Nature
Morning Glory, Colorado Story

Cindy Burgess Travel
Where Are The Waves?

Gloria L. Green Travel
Hoover Dam Vista

Melanie Cragg   Nature
A Morning In Maine

Bernice Tessman   Travel
Bridging The Way Over Peaceful Waters

Belinda Brehm Enkro   Nature
Sunset On Wilson Lake

Arthur Bye   Nature
European Beech Trees

Carol J. Hawk   Travel
Grand Canyon

Lilian V. Sweeney Lillian   Nature
Autumn Splendor

Yvette Dumont Connell   Nature
Sunset

James F. Barron IV   Travel
Alpen Glanz

Fred Van Hook   Nature
Arizona Splendor

Kenneth Shain   Travel
Signal In The Storm—Woodmont, CT

Lisa Levesque   Nature
Levant's Early Light

Thelma Angell   Travel
Sunset In Hawaii

Melvin Lapp   Nature
Vacation In The Tetons

Allen Young   People
Evacuation Of Vietnam

Bob Dalton   Travel
Looking Through The Eyes Of God

Gregg Persons   Children
Four Cute Kids

Linda Snyder   Animals/Pets
American Beauty

Charles Lockhart   Animals/Pets
Bouye 2000

Michel Miller   Animals/Pets
Don't Worry, We're Not Your New Neighbors

Katie Chandler   Nature
Serenity

James Edward Heiberg   Sports
Waiting To Race

Janice Kozen   Travel
Easter Procession

Rachelle Peck   Children
Untitled

Pauline Sutton   Animals/Pets
Fishing Buddies

Shukura K. Crooke   Nature
America's Paradise

Holly M. Bailey   Animals/Pets
Bosom Buddies

Heather Deheney   Nature
The Great Oak

Susan Milner   Children
Halloween, Pipi Longstocking

Enis Pinar   Travel
Spring Morning On The Inn

Tammy S. Blankenship   Children
Takin' A Break

Wanda Steele Nature
Plains Sunset

Kathy Sain Nature
A View To Remember

Jennifer Giuliano Animals/Pets
Mattie's Road Trip

Yvonne F. Correa Nature
Desert In Bloom

Amy Demar Nature
Silhouetted Sunset

Barb Horgan Animals/Pets
Pals

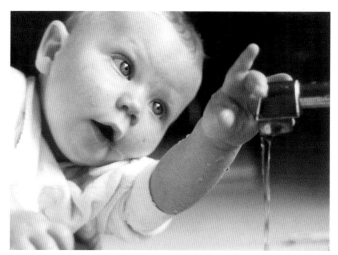

Dianne M. Fertig   Children
Discovering Water

Diane McGill   Children
Wedding Afterthoughts

Laray Dillman   Children
Unwilling Playmate

Larry L. Bobseine   Nature
The Lord Is My Shepherd

Joan Gribben   Children
Smiling Friends

Elizabeth Wanjura   Children
The Doll Doctor

Joan Lademann   Animals/Pets
Tiger Keeping The Coffee Warm

Morris Sauter   Nature
Superstitious Light

Becky Blackwell   Nature
Serenity With A Splash

Gary A. Wright   Children
Frosty And Friends

Albert W. McMahan   Animals/Pets
How's My Tan?

Annette Sokoll   Nature
Feathered Friend

Les Mills   Portraiture
My Culture, My Fashion

Julia Owens   Children
Kissing Cousins

C. Weir Horswill   Other
Ice Storm's Beauty

Tammy Elrick   Nature
God's Evening Splendor

Karen L. Humphriss   Animals/Pets
Super Catch, Rommel

Jeffrey K. Poznick   Nature
Morning Web

Sarah Shin Animals/Pets
City Life

Michael Alvich Animals/Pets
A Golden Moment—LuLu And Duke

Patrick McMullen Sports
A Great Victory

Sarah L. Flowers Animals/Pets
Got Heart?

Marjorie J. White Animals/Pets
A Rose Among The Daisies

R. Christner Travel
Cocoa Beach Sunrise

Grace Marquiss   Children
Deep In Thought

Thomas Noethlich   Children
Bowl Of Trouble

Valerie Douglas   Nature
Seals At La Jolla

Harry Reiner   Animals/Pets
My Babies

Barbara Stolp   Children
It's Somebody's Birthday

Arianna Sbraccia   Children
Rub-A-Dub-Tub, Twins In A Tub

Becky Baune   Children
Look, Mom

Holly Crabtree   People
Kissing Cousins

Helen T. Maly   Children
Doing His Homework

Ron Isakson   Children
Jacob's Shadow

Becky Simmons   Children
Hey! My Name's Not Bossy!

Stephenie Sporer   Children
First Halloween

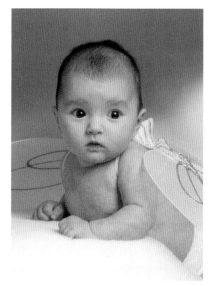

Emelina Rodriguez   Children
Perfect Angel

Rose Quint   Nature
The Beauty Of Mother Nature

Carolyn S. Guilfoyle   Animals/Pets
Asha's Angels

Colette Osmun   Animals/Pets
Titan In Pig Costume

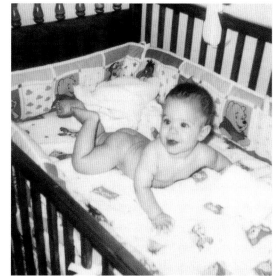

Mary Wessel   Children
How Do I Look, Granny?

Patricia Martin   Animals/Pets
Puppy Love

Janet Kitten   Children
Too Much Fun At The Backyard Beach

Joan Shanholtz   Animals/Pets
Oh No! I Messed Up The Christmas Card Pictures

Khristie Engberg   People
Big Rock Hike

Virginia Preston   Animals/Pets
Blue Eye Bandit Waiting For His Date

Margie Seaton   Children
Child Smelling Flowers

Jason Taylor   Nature
Liquid Sky

Charles Crooks   Animals/Pets
Our Precious Kittens

Jonathan Black   Children
Who, Me!

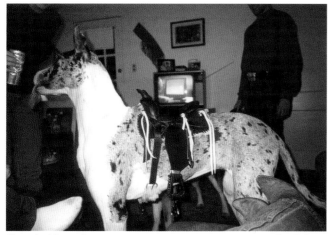

Donnie Alexander   Animals/Pets
Don't Drink And Ride

Mandy Garza   Other
Railroad

Arnold W. Ehrsam   Other
Reflections

Nathan Stevens   Nature
Goodbye Romance

Christine Nolan   Animals/Pets
Which Way Did That Squirrel Go?

Sonja G. Kennedy   Nature
Plains Sunset

Luke Clay Butara   Children
Terrible Threes

Ron Lapp   Nature
Roses

Michael Harrop   Nature
Catch Of The Day

Stella Rubilar   Travel
Polar Bear Adventure

Barbara Smith   Nature
Sunrise

Kate Mortimer   Animals/Pets
Sri Lankan Macaque Monkey

Lisa Trinh   Children
Baby Tiffany In A Traditional Chinese Outfit

Jeannette Hamilton   Animals/Pets
Christmas Wishes

Kay Driscoll   Animals/Pets
Purrrfectly Content

Thomas R. Reed Sr.   Children
Grandmother Mitzi Layne Meets Grandson Joseph Reed

Judy Connell   Animals/Pets
Closeness Is Priceless

Amanda J. Berry   Animals/Pets
High-Flying Britts

Jean Brown   Animals/Pets
Grrrr, Mine—Just Try Taking It!

Angie Turano   Other
Even A Cat Gets Sick

Wanda J. Koczur   Children
Oh Yeah!

Kisha Smith   Children
Angel Of Mine

Lorraine Buckmaster   Animals/Pets
This Is The Famous Guilt Trip!

Wade McCraw   Children
Christmas '98

Tonya L. Brady   Nature
Late Evening At Turks Pond

Bruce Dunn   Children
Rainy Day Rachel

Lynn S. Webb   Children
Will's First Picnic

Myrtle H. Stone   Nature
African Gold Crown

Anne M. Quinto   Other
Got Mail?

Lisa Wood   Children
Here's Looking At You, Kid

Gerry Meyers   Children
Daniel

Rehina Rodriguez   Nature
A Storm Coming

Herb Buchite   Nature
Serenity At Day's End

Jan Pinkerton   Animals/Pets
The Little Colonel

Mellany J. Johnson   Nature
Sentry On Duty

Gilda Hoopes   Children
Brothers Forever

Eric Doerrer   Children
Ty

Ronald E. Bourne   Other
Imitation Of Nature

Michelle Zielinski   Animals/Pets
Me And My Teddy

Gino Losenno   Nature
Changing Form

Charles J. Anderson   Travel
Miners Castle

Joy D'Uva   Children
Cheeky Girl

Karey Dichtel   Animals/Pets
The Double Wood

Richard Glenn   Nature
Alabama Hills, Long Pine, CA

Dale Tulloch   Nature
Bear

Dodi Callanan   Nature
Solitude

Barb Deale Animals/Pets
Prissy Dee Bar

Pam Petersen Children
Future Gymnast

Nicole Rosenlund Nature
Day Moon

Leticia Preciado Children
Sweet Harvest

Reba Kimbler Nature
Dinnertime

Denise Bates Other
Summer Relaxation

N. F. Krebs   Action
Is It Real Or Supernatural?

Jack A. Hartzell   Animals/Pets
Oh Boy! It's Time For The Game!

Hector Perez   Children
Tired Little Princess

Sarah Haines   Children
The Great Pumpkin

Gail Smith   Nature
Early Autumn At Bent Creek

George J. Marshall   Children
What? Am I Boring You?

Cynthia C. Wongsurawat   Animals/Pets
Waiting Patiently For Dinner

Thais Streeter   Sports
Look At That Fish

Phil McInturf   Animals/Pets
Catnap Vest And Hat

Lucille Blankenship   Nature
Tranquility

Connie Brady   Animals/Pets
We're Outta Here

R. Allen Shotwell   Children
Matthew And Grandma Waiting For Sister, Amanda

ARTISTS'
PROFILES

AURAN

A combination of history, travel, and nostalgia made this opportune autumn day a real treasure. A Washington "Arlingtonian" for many years, I was glad that the beautiful colors of autumn were right around home.

ABRAMS, BETH

I am very interested in making photography my life's work. I continually frame everyday things as if I was setting up a photographic image. I am currently a high school senior, and I plan to study photography next fall at a university. I am presently fascinated by photographing nature. My photograph "Sunset" is one of my favorite pictures so far.

ADAM, SUZETTE M.

Angel came to us at about 2 weeks old. Her mother did not want her, and she had a hernia about the size of a hard boiled egg. She fit in the palm of my hand. We bottle fed her and she had surgery for the hernia at about 5 weeks old. She is a survivor. That's why we call her our little angel. She is 2 years old now and is what they call pleasantly plump.

ADAMS, BOB

My interest in photography originated with my father, Robert W. Adams. Dad was an aerial photographer with the Army Air Corps in World War II, and has cultivated my photographic talent since childhood. This is a photo of one of my dearest friends, Michael Patterson. An all-around super human being, this aspiring model is a truly beautiful person in every way. It is my honor to have taken his first published photo, but certainly not his last!

ADKINS, MARIE

I love cats and photography! Even while sleeping, cats never stop posing. Their insatiable curiosity, flowing form, beautiful expressive eyes, and quiet, graceful ways make them my favorite subject. Coco came to live on our Indiana farm several years ago. He was special from the start. At bedtime he shares my pillow, snoring softly and barely moving a whisker all night. Since he rarely climbs, I was lucky to catch him up a tree—especially on a day when the sky matched his eyes.

AKERS, KATHERINE

My small 35mm camera is most always with me. As an amateur, it is exciting to photograph my grandchildren, garden club events, church activities, animals, water scenes, etc. "Grateful Kiss" was made during a walk through a large horse stable in West Virginia. In a corner of the stable, I was thrilled to witness this endearing show of care and affection.

ALBERTINE, OLGA

Have you ever wondered what your cat thinks about? Is he staring at a bird, or another cat across the way? Our cat is like our child. My husband, Mike, and I love Oscar as if he was a child. Some people have baby picture books; we have our cat's picture book. We have always taken pictures of our Oscar. There are more pictures of Oscar than there are of us.

ALDRICH, SARAH

This is a picture of my family's favorite place to visit: Perkins Cove. I am a first-year photography student, but I have always enjoyed taking pictures of various vacations spots. I chose this photo because looking at it reminds me of the fun times and beautiful scenery of Maine.

ALEXANDER, ANDREA

My family and I visited Anna Ruby Falls in October of 1999; that was when the picture was taken. I loved the natural way the trees fell when the hurricane passed, the way the leaves fell perfectly on the rocks, and the coolness of the moss and water. Nature is one of the most beautiful things to photograph.

ALLEN, LEE

This is a picture of my son, who is my dream come true. He is 7 weeks old here. It was Halloween Day and he's wearing his "Boo" outfit. This was one of his first few smiles and laughs, and I was able to capture it in a picture.

ALLOWAY, LINDA

I love animals, and I love taking photographs. The two mix very well any time, any place, everywhere.

AMANN, WILLIAM

The beauty in the eye of this beholder lies in the portraiture of a universal aspiration of youngsters to "keep step" with their heroes. In this case, it is a show of patriotism with the soldier. The scene is in Red Square, Moscow, by the then-revered tomb wherein Lenin's body lies preserved as a national monument. The photo was taken in 1966, during the Cold War. One had to be careful in what could be photographed with impunity. We can speculate that these boys grew up to be soldiers in the Russian contingent of peacekeepers in Kosovo, or they did they grow up as warring militants in Chechnya?

ANDERSON, DEBBIE L.

This photo was taken in our home by my mother, Linda Hanzlik. Our cats have been a great joy and wonderful friends to us. I would like to urge everyone to get their pets from a Humane Society shelter and ask everyone to give generously to the Humane Society.

ANDERSON, JENI

To the two greatest people in the world, who love me so much. This is for you two and all the love a little girl could ever give. Thank you for always being there.

ARNOLD, MARILYN

We live in Ohio and were visiting my husband, Daniel's, daughter and family in Woodstock, GA, on Easter. When we arrived back to their home after church, I asked our granddaughters, Latisha and Sonala Wolfe, if I could take their picture in their pretty dresses before they changed into play clothes. Grandpa and I bought the dresses on our honeymoon six years ago. I told them to act like they liked each other. The picture tells the rest of story.

ASBURY, MICHAEL ROBERT

My Lord and savior has graced my life in so many ways; I'm extremely happy to be able to capture

the beauty that he's created and bring it to you. This image was taken outside of Mawitou Springs, CO, close to the "garden of the Gods." The aura of the picture also reflects the personality of the people that reside there—solid, strong, and lovely. I was so moved by the region that I plan to make it my home. Special thanks to my Lord for the angels He's sent, and special thanks to Helga for the pick.

ASKOAK, ANGELINA

This photo was taken in October 1999. The view was very beautiful and looked like a peaceful place to be. This mountain is located approximately two hundred miles upriver from the mouth of the Yukon River and about seven miles northeast of Russian Mission. This area brings in summer activities, such as boating, picnics, berry picking, fishing, and hunting. I think that this is the most scenic mountain in the whole Yukon Delta area.

ATKINSON, PAMELA

I am a certified yoga teacher and have always felt very connected to Mother Nature. I've always been fascinated with how the sun kisses the ocean good night and the ocean answers with its roar while the seagulls sing along. It's quite a symphony. I have also been fascinated with Mother Nature's painter's palette and the colors of the flowers, grass, trees, and skies. This is how "Heavenly Gifts" was created: by the truly awesome artist, Mother Nature, and my deep connection to her. It was a moment to behold, and I wanted to share it with the world and capture it with my camera.

AUMEND, DEVIN

I am 15 years old and enjoy experimenting with photography. I usually try to plan my shots, which include people, scenic, and sometimes action photos. This shot, however, could never be planned. Lucky for me, this young hawk decided to kill a rabbit in my yard and was too immature to realize that he could have picked it up and flown away to eat in private, thus giving me this once-in-a-lifetime shot! I have to say, I was afraid to get so close for this picture, because he definitely expressed his displeasure at my being there. But he wasn't about to give up his meal for anything!

AYERS, GENEVIEVE

When my husband, an avid photographer, passed away, he left me his Olympus BM2. I always take it with me on my visits to my children. This photo is of my granddaughter Eva. Her project in the 4-H club is raising chickens. I took this picture of her collecting eggs from under the chicken coupe her father made for her project.

BABCOCK, KAREN

This is a photo of our 11-year-old diabetic cocker spaniel. Between him and our two little granddaughters, our camera is always within reach. We had wanted Courtney to wear the hat, but she kept pulling it off. Gus happened to be sitting there, so I plopped it on his head and took the shot. That's all it took. Courtney put on the hat and wore it the rest of the morning. The fact that Gus has cataracts helped his impression of the long night.

I love capturing these memory moments to enjoy over and over.

BACK, STEVEN R.
I was at the new zoo in Green Bay, WI. The drumming could be heard throughout the zoo. As I grew closer, the prairie chicken didn't miss a beat, and I didn't miss the chance to get the shot.

BANKS, STACEY
Children like this one are my favorite things to shoot photos of. I live in Gallant, AL, and have a growing interest in taking shots of babies and children that you can't get in a studio. What made this one special to me is that the little boy is a very quiet and shy child, but when I dressed him like a cowboy he fell right into the role and still had an angelic face of innocence.

BARDEN, VIVIAN
From my porch I have a lovely view of the Potomac river. Early one morning while enjoying my first cup of coffee, I saw the sun literally rise up out of the water. I was fascinated! I knew I had to have a picture. After many tries, I think my picture fully captures the beauty of the sunrise. The sun is in this position for a short time once a year, so I am pleased to have this scene on film.

BASEHORE, GINNY
As a retired grandmother of four, I now have more time to take photos. This was only the fourth game I could attend, and when the fog rolled in, I could not resist. I hope I have more opportunities to capture more exciting shots like this in the future.

BATES, CHRISTINE
I have always enjoyed taking pictures. Completing a course in photography has given me the opportunity to enhance my photography. Thus, the darling barn at Waters Farm, Sutton, MA, was captured on film. This barn had originally stood in Manchaug, a nearby town. It was then disassembled and moved by horse-drawn wagons to Waters Farm. It remained there six years until a large crew of volunteers held a ham raising. It now houses antique farm implements and carriages.

BAUNE, BECKY
This photo will forever be my favorite. She is my life—my daughter, Jessica Maria. She has a great love of life and love for all of God's little creatures. I will cherish this moment in time for the rest of eternity. It will continue to remind me of the innocence in all of our children. Just after my grandmother, Maria Senger's, funeral, Jessica brought this toad to me and asked if I thought Grandma Senger would like to have it, so we brought it to her at the cemetery.

BAZYDOLA, BERNARD J.
This photo was taken during a trip to Eastern Europe. I am an amateur baker, gardener, and photographer—not necessarily in that order. I began taking photos while in the USMC, United State Marine Corps. Over the years, I have found less is more in photos to be appreciated. My subjects are as varied as landscapes, wildlife, flora, and fauna, as well as people. My photos, many of which I have on display in my home, serve as reminders of my past experiences in life and moments of enjoyment.

BEARDSLEY, LAURA
This is a photo of my dog Ricky Gayth Beardsley going to a Halloween party. I just happened to catch his normally devilish personality. Although my main profession is as a figure-skating coach, I love spending time with my two shelties and taking pictures of them and any other unusual images.

BENSON, NANCY
This is a picture of my husband, Roger, enjoying a Key West, FL, sunset. We enjoy travelling, and I take a lot of pictures along the way. I've never entered a photography contest before, so this is very exciting and encouraging to me as an amateur photographer. Our twelve grandchildren will enjoy seeing their grandpa's picture in "Eye Of The Beholder."

BERRIS, ELLEN
Citabria's second birthday was a milestone in her life. Born with a heart defect, she wasn't expected to live past two. Surgery was a success and she will live a long, happy life with us. Cessna is struggling with her heart disease that will eventually take her life. She has given us ten years of joy, unconditional love, and happiness. We feel so fortunate to have shared her life for so many wonderful years. My husband, Herschel, and I are pilots, so Cessna and Citabria have truly completed our lives and our family.

BETTFREUND, JOHN
I like to take pictures and have done so for years. I watched the mother hummingbird build this nest, lay two eggs, and then hatch two babies. I watched them being fed and grow. The bird on left flew away first, and the one on the right left the next day. A regular silver dollar will cover this nest, since these are really little fellows.

BINGER, JUDITH
I am a photographer, like my mother was. My mother died recently, and I will always remember her and the pictures she took. I have been entering photo contests and I have won some. I won the cameras I took them with. I am retired from Social Security. I do volunteer work at the Humane Society of Greater Kansas City, which is where I took the picture. The two kittens were playing with a play toy. They are brothers, and they were adopted by an older man the next week after the picture was taken. I wish I could adopt a dog or cat.

BISHOP, ANN M.
During forty-seven years of the fifty-two years that my husband and I have been married, I have filled umpteen photo albums of our four children. We have always felt poignancy behind this picture of our shy 2½-year-old Sandy kissing the nose of our friends' very beautiful daughter, who is eloquently named Paris, on the beach of Cape May, NJ, during the summer of 1958. It is a moment of life's sweet innocence!

BLOMSETH, CARLA
Autumn is my favorite time of the year, and there is nowhere more breathtaking than the Rocky Mountains in the fall. I was driving through the San Juan Mountains with friends when I noticed the amazing blue sky with the aspens glittering above. I enjoy frequent getaways to experiment with photography. My career as a pharmacist can be demanding, and I've found that photography can be relaxing as well as rewarding.

BOESGAARD, PATTI
Since I had my children, Heather and Paul, I began taking many pictures. I have to see what I can do with the camera. It goes with me just about everywhere. Fall is such a pretty time of year. We visit Vermont frequently, and, as usual, my family rides around with me so I can take some pictures. This beautiful tree with its gold leaves caught my attention. I was surprised how well it turned out!

BOGAN, MARCELLA
Amber is my great-granddaughter, who I was babysitting. While I was busy and my attention wasn't on her, she took off for the other room and positioned herself at the organ, ready to play. I couldn't resist the shot. I'm no photographer, but I thought the snap was really good and a great memory for her of her great-grandma.

BOISJOLI, TAMMIE
Every spring, one of the most photographed places in Europe comes to life. Keukenhof Gardens is located in Lisse, Holland, near Amsterdam. My husband, Ron, and I made the gardens an annual visit while living in Europe for a few years. My sister, Tracye, and her friend were visiting us on this particular trip in April 1999. We felt this was one of the most beautiful sights in the gardens. It truly looks like a flowing river. The colors are so vivid due to the typically overcast European skies. Keukenhof Gardens is a photographer's dream.

BORGER, DOROTHY J.
My friend in the chair is Poco. I am a retired teacher, and I have worked as an accountant and an x-ray technician in the past. I spent fifteen months as x-ray technician in Nome, AK, in the 1960s.

BOSNAK, SONDAE
I took up photography as a hobby over twenty years ago. It has always been a relaxing and fulfilling pastime for me. Every photo is unique in it's own right. This photo was taken in Shawnee, PA, in a small town near the Delaware Water Gap. They have a balloon festival that takes place every autumn. This event is always very exhilarating and beautiful. To see the balloons' amazing colors and nature's magnificent autumn shades is quite majestic. As you can see from this photo, I was at the actual opening of the balloon as they inflated it with air from the fan. The shadow is another balloonist attending to the topmost of the balloon. I guess you can say I was at the right place at the right time.

BOURNE, RONALD E.
We all look at the clouds and see different things depicted in our minds. This was taken on board the carnival ship "Inspiration," off the Caribbean isle of Cirenada while en route to Puerto Rico. Being an amateur photographer for many years, I could not resist taking this picture. It is just anoth-

er thing that we see in the clouds; some things never change.

BOVO, KATHLEEN
This is a photo taken in my backyard of two of my grandsons. They love using my umbrella to play with. I was tending them one day and had the sprinklers on. I let them use my umbrella and decided to take a picture. I'm always taking pictures of my grandchildren. Their dad is a photographer and has done school pictures, year book photos, weddings, and family photos. He owns a children's photo store called Kiddie Kandids that is in several malls in the mountain west. He complimented me on this photo, so I decided to turn it in for the contest. I love to share photos with family and friends. They are very appreciative to have pictures of events that they might not capture because they left their cameras home. My grandchildren love to see themselves in funny shots, and I am making photo books for them individually. I recently bought a photography book and hope to learn how to take better pictures. My husband, Rich, and I have eight children and four grandchildren so far. I have been a nurse for twenty-nine years and still love caring for others.

BOWMAN, ALICE C.
This was taken one very early morning when my brother Tony and my sister-in-law Pat were visiting from Indiana. I've always enjoyed the beauty of nature and the serenity of early morning—my time for my creator. I'm the seventh of eight children, and I was born in Indiana. I have four children, five stepchildren, and sixteen grandchildren.

BOWMAN, CARL
My brother-in-law and I will do crazy things to make our wives and his two daughters laugh. When we are together having fun, we forget about the everyday problems that occur around us. The six of us have a love between us that I wish all people had for each other.

BRADY, TONYA L.
I am a 55-year-old housewife from Springfield, CO. I was so surprised and very proud to learn that my photo had advanced to semi-finalist in your photo contest. My husband, Ora, and I fish at Turks Pond in the summer, and if my photo was recognized I wanted everyone to enjoy some of the beauty of Baca County. "Late Evening At Turks Pond" truly is in the eye of the beholder. Thank you.

BRASSFIELD, ROBIN J.
This was taken out front of a little church when I was visiting my mother, Sheila Smalley, in Williams, OR. My mother and I both carry our cameras in our purses everywhere we go. This is one big reason why. There are so many precious animals out there. I have six dogs and thousands of pictures of them; I will share one of them next time. This little tabby kitten was so cute and determined to make this doe share that she did not stop holding her until the doe was through eating all of the cottage cheese. Then she only got to lick the container. Too cute.

BRATZ, PAULA
This is a photo of my son, Nicholas, at the age of 2

years. He had just had a swimming lesson, which both excited and overwhelmed him. I caught the essence of his mental critique in this photo.

BRAUBITZ, VIVIAN
This photo of my husband, Charles, was taken while we were on vacation. He was holding the hand of my great-niece, Jacquie, while enjoying the sunset at Cape Breton, Nova Scotia. I was hanging back waiting to shoot at the right moment, and when I looked into the view-finder and realized they had stepped into the view, I knew I had captured a unique moment. It was an unforgettable encounter, and I was ecstatic when I saw the results. Being an archaeologist has helped me develop a keen eye for detail and an appreciation of the vast grandeur of nature.

BRAWDY, JOHN A.
This is a picture of our dog, Sheba, and our cat, Minnie, with the rest of the family celebrating Sheba's fourth birthday. We celebrate our pets' birthdays just like the rest of the family, except they get a cupcake with a candle. Our pets are very special to us; we love them just like our kids.

BRECKENRIDGE, JUDITH E.
In August of 1998, I took my children, Amber, 5 and Andrew, 6, to Morro Bay. They were so excited and ran ahead of me on the sand. I had my camera ready, and when I caught up to them, I found them holding on to each other in total awe of the vast Pacific Ocean and the waves. It was a cold, overcast day in Morro Bay in contrast to the heat wave back home in Winton. I always have film in my camera ready to record my life in photographs. This is my first contest.

BRESCH, CHERYL
This is a photo of my 2-year-old daughter, Samantha. I took this picture three weeks after she was diagnosed with cancer. Taking pictures became a part of our lives along with chemotherapy, doctor visits, and hospital stays. I wanted to save every precious moment. When I didn't think that I could go on another day, I would look at this picture and see her pain, anger, and courage. If she could go on, so could I. Two and a half years later, she is cancer free. We both made it.

BRIGANCE, VIRGINIA
A short holiday on Padre Island was the destination of his parents, Mike and Paula. Granny was supposed to be in charge, but all she seemed to do was snap pictures of her first grandson. Landry's brilliant brown eyes searched the space of the toy-strewn family room, and he moved swiftly to claim his trophy. Granddad was an easy target as he slumbered in the sleepy blue chair, dreaming of fat cows responding to the crisp bite of the diligent cattle dog he loved so much. He could almost feel it.

BROOKS, GEORGE H.
Sunrises and sunsets are special moments in time around the world. They mark the beginning of a new day or the end of a day's journey. This sunset was taken in the final moments of an hour's time spent shooting a roll of film of the scene while watching for the "right moment" and won-

dering whether John Coulter, the first white man to see this area, had seen such a sunset.

BROWN, GLADYS
My husband, Bruce, had taken me to the park for relaxation while I was recuperating from an illness. I took my camera, since it was fall and my favorite subjects are seasons of the year, sunrises, and sunsets. I was fortunate enough to experience the glorious colors, and I wanted to capture them.

BROWN, MARK A.
As an amateur astronomer, one of my favorite pastimes is observing and photographing the moon from my own backyard. On this particular evening, I found myself marvelling at the moon's large disk hanging motionless over the horizon. The moon looks enormous when compared to familiar objects or backgrounds such as distant trees, a house, or a city skyline. It is one of nature's most powerful illusions. This is a photograph of the Tower of America in San Antonio, TX, superimposed on top of the full moon, depicting such an illusion.

BUCHANAN, HAL M.
Photography has been a hobby for most of my adult life. I have enjoyed capturing the sights of my travels during twenty-one years in the US Navy and taking candid shots of friends, family, and family pets. No member of the family is a professional, but we all have the desire to take that "perfect" picture. In the case of my yellow lab, Beau, it is the subject that makes this photo so special, not the photographer. His true character and personality just jump out at you in their photo. What a loving rasputin my "helper" can be!

BUCHHOLZ, BARBARA
While vacationing in Georgia, we stopped at a petting farm near Stone Mountain. There were deer, goats, squirrels, and chipmunks to see. Just as we approached a red barn, three noses poked out a window. We just laughed, and I snapped this photo. They were begging for fresh veggies and "Another Carrots Please!" I am a dental assistant. In my spare time, I enjoy taking photos of my three cats and vacationing in Florida with my husband, Michael.

BURDESHAW, KEVIN
I am so fortunate to relive the wonders of childhood through my daughter, Lilith Mae. Every day is awash with discovery and magic. Each moment is full of joy and amazement, and each experience is another fantastic part of the puzzle we call life. Sometimes we take for granted the small miracles of everyday: the sun on our face, the wind in our hair, or water as it gently runs between our fingers. Life is beautiful when observed through the eyes of a child.

BURLEIGH, GLENDA
This is a picture of my husband, Garry. He is blind, as you can see by the white cane he is holding. He is standing at the end of the "River Walk" bridge in Chattanooga, TN. As he stood there waiting for me to take a few photographs, I looked down the bridge and captured this unique shot. Photography has always been a passion of mine. I guess you could call me a serious amateur photographer.

BURNS, LYNNE
My husband and I lived on a farm in Indiana with our three boys and many animals for fourteen years. Over the years we took numerous photos of animals. This has always been one of our favorites. I adopted the kitten from a local shelter. She was about four weeks old at the time this photo was taken. We have recently purchased a home on the intracoastal water way in North Carolina. I am looking forward to photographing dolphins while sitting on our dock.

BURRIS, LEE
I took this photo on a camping trip in Mississippi. The front of my tent faced a small clearing of trees that lined the lake. It was the first light of a warm spring morning. The first thing I saw as I exited my tent was a father and son casting their lines. I grabbed my camera, having time for only one shot before they drifted out of view.

BURSESE, KATHERINE
This is a portrait of our wonderful rottweiler, "Carly," who we rescued from certain death on January 2, 1998. She is truly an angel with paws. She is pictured here with my husband, Larry, this past fall of 1999. The look in her eyes shows the depth of her love and devotion to us.

BUSCHINSKY, MARIE-LOUISE
All of my animals have been rescued. I want to believe Moxie and Munchkin have something to laugh about every day in their new home with me—especially now that they have a rescued German shepherd brother named Wrong Way Corrigan. My joy is in watching and photographing their celebration of life.

BYE, ARTHUR
I am a landscape architect who for half a century has been photographing nature. "European Beech Trees" was included in a book that I wrote about moods in landscape, which pertains to the emotional qualities that one can find in the natural landscape. Some examples of these qualities are: mysterious, serene, grotesque, friendly, humorous, and many more.

CARD, STELLA C.
My nephews are twins, Stephen and Nicholas, who like to play ball with their father. Here is one twin determined to swing at the ball. I take photos for enjoyment but wanted to share this child's determination. Did he hit the ball? Of course.

CARNIVAL, MELVA
I grew up on a farm in Ohio. Now I live with my husband and two sons in Orlando, FL. Each year, our family travels to Ohio for some good old fashioned summertime fun complete with a tire swing under the big maple tree, creek beds flowing with tadpoles, and newborn baby animals. This photo is of my youngest son, Kyle, with his cousins in the background. Although we live in the suburbs, spending time in the country leaves us with memories and experiences unsurpassed by none other. This is truly one of my many favorite photos.

CARR, LORIE
This is a photo of one of the many historic buildings that stand along Lake Michigan Little Sable.

We have forgotten what history and present day use these beautiful buildings bring. Each year my family and I take a week and travel along Michigan in search of a different lighthouse. The view from the top of Big Sable is breathtaking. Once you have walked along the sandy beach and felt the presence of its being, then can you understand the meaning of, "I am the light in the storm." My husband, Terry, is a supervisor, and I am a lab technician. We have three children: Ashley, 14; Anthony, 13; and Jared, 8.

CARROLL, BRIAN
The "Best Buds" in this picture are actually Brenden and Caitlin, who are stepbrother and sister. Both were 7 years old at the time of the picture and on summer vacation for 1999, down at the Jersey Shore L.B.I. The beautiful sunset glistening off the bay in the background adds to the glow in the faces of the constant companions and best buds.

CARROLL, KAREN
This is my daughter Christa admiring a new puppy while I'm admiring her. Christa is our oldest, and is now out on her own and misses animals when at home in her apartment, so she loves every moment there is with an animal around.

CARSWELL, EARL
"Some Like It Hot" was birthed out of my fondness for hot, spicy, Southern cuisine coupled with a desire to create a unique photograph. I've enjoyed photography as a hobby since 1968. My other favorite hobbies include golf and bass fishing.

CARTWRIGHT, MARY E. S.
I love to swim. My husband, Dan, and I bought a house with an in-ground pool. After our son, Levi, was born, we thought it was best that he learn early to swim. He has been taking lessons since he was 8 months old. Summers seem short in Buffalo, NY, so I picked up an underwater camera to capture summertime fun. Levi, at 3 years and 8 months old, wanted me to photograph his underwater swimming he learned from his cousin, Haley, that summer of 1999. This picture is my most cherished memory of "My Water Baby."

CASEY, ARLENE J.
I went with my husband to a fly-in breakfast. The airport cat paid no attention to the people walking along the flight line behind him, but stayed focused on the rodent hole.

CASLAKE, SANDRA
My husband, Alan, and I do a lot of traveling. We love the outdoors and the beauty of nature. Our camera is always with us, which was well worth it on this day. This photo was captured between Golden and Revelstoke of British Columbia. For that little bit of a second, it looked like the goat standing on top by itself was saying, "This land is mine. I'm the king of this castle!" I personally feel very lucky to have witnessed this moment in time.

CHAIN, LAWANDA
This is one of those once-in-a-lifetime photos. I was standing at the end of our runway, when my husband, Neal, took off in his spray plane. I knew as soon as I snapped it that I had something special!

CHANGACHIT, TIEMCHAN
On November 25, 1999, I bought a cornish hen, and I stuffed and stuffed with stuffing until the hen stood up on the plate. I looked at it and laughed and laughed. Then I grabbed a camera. I took a picture and then put the stuffed hen in the oven until it was done. Here comes my Thanksgiving dinner.

CHARLES, PRISCILLA
My husband, Loonie, and I own and operate a variety store on Route 49 in Bridgeton, NJ, where Buddy is our partner. This is a photo of Loonie and the "World's Best Partner," our 145 pound shepherd-husky named Buddy. Buddy thinks he is human and brings much joy in our lives and the lives of all who meet him. Besides these two loves of my life, photography is another love. I get much joy in taking pictures of many beautiful subjects, sights, and events in life.

CHASE, KELLY L.
This picture reminds me of Pink Floyd's The Wall lyrics: "We don't need no education, all in all we're just another brick in the wall." The professors in this photo disprove those lyrics. They are committed, dedicated professionals who teach future educators how important educational design is. They do not treat their students as just another "brick in the wall," but take an interest in helping each of us to become the best teacher that we can become. Our students have individual, special needs. The people in this photo have treated us as individuals, that we may become special educators.

CHEN, DAVE
The essence of this photograph taken in the San Juan Islands, captures the underlying bond between humans and animals, the gift of life. The secret being shared was that my wife, Jodi, was six months pregnant with our twin boys. The beauty of this picture, to me, is surpassed only by the elegance of the lives captured in this scene— the three that are visible and our two unborn sons. Beauty truly is in the eye of the beholder.

CHENG, STEPHANIE
Mini is from Costa Rica. She is half bichon frise and half poodle. While on vacation in Costa Rica, my family and I fell in love with a dog similar to Mini. We decided to bring home a dog with us back to New York, so we went to the same breeder. We went through so much to get her papers and permission to board her on the phone. But all in all, it was worth it.

CHISARIK, JUDITH
This is a photo of my granddaughter, Emily. She loves to wear my straw hat and play in our garden. She has a little sister, Kaitlyn. Her parents are Stephen and Lori. My husband, Steve, and I love sharing photos of our grandchildren.

CHIVERS, TERRI
I am a fourth grade teacher who combines the love of nature with the love of photography. This shot was taken at one of our family's favorite hiking spots in the Vintah mountains. Autumn is the most beautiful time of year with the many colors that are displayed in these canyons. It is a tradi-

tion each year for me to collect beautiful autumn leaves to display in my classroom, as well as sharing my photographs with my students.

CHMIDLING, DIANNE

Dianne Chmidling was born and raised in the midwest. This photo represents two subjects close to Dianne's heart—children and the Amish heritage. These children are really cousins, with Becca's bonnet falling back as she gives her beloved cousin, Justin, a little kiss. Taken in Kansas country, these beautiful children represent the simple life of beautiful Amish heritage. Dianne's other interests include horseback riding with her husband, vintage button collecting, and selling on Internet auctions. She is the director of training for a community bank in Kansas and holds degree in education and management. A favorite reminder: "Video tape your parents' laughter."

CHRISTENSEN, JANE

A couple of years ago when I was visiting my mother, she had two litters of kittens in the house. Bridgette, the dog pictured, noticed that the mother of this kitten had rejected him because he was so sick and weak. Bridgette adopted him. She carried him by mouth, cleaned him, and slept with him, so I had no choice but to bring him home. This is not the first time Bridgette has mothered a sick child. She has slept with sick piglets and baby chicks as well. She is the "Mother Of All The Things," and I love her.

CHURCH, MEGAN

Taking pictures is both a fulfilling and relaxing hobby for me. Each picture has the potential of telling its own story. I took this one my senior year in high school as kind of a joke on my friend. When I got the picture back, she and I were both surprised at how well it turned out. The depth within the photo seems to tell a story of its own.

CLARK, LARRY

This picture was taken on a rainy day while the sun was shining across the lake. A huge and beautiful rainbow spread across the sky, but seeing this sunset with the darkened clouds was something else. I grew up on Silver Lake. At first I only stayed in the summer months, and now I stay all year with my wife, Leah, who says, "You can never have enough sunset pictures." I enjoy being outside with nature and wildlife. It is forever changing.

CLOSE, SABRA

After moving from the city to a farm in Iowa, I began a lifelong dream of collecting animals, or pets, rather. Chickens, ducks, peacocks, sheep, goats, cats, dogs, pot-bellied pigs—you name it. Then I just began taking their pictures to share with friends and family, although I must have over a hundred myself. Choosing just one was the hardest part. But I've always liked this one of my "pound" cat, Tyrone, and was thrilled and surprised that it was chosen.

COCHRAN, KELLY L.

My work as a nurse has helped me to believe that some memories truly do last a lifetime. While working with the elderly, I have had the pleasure of hearing many stories of the past, and most of these stories come from one glance at an old photo. Over the years, photography has become my favorite hobby. This photo was shot near St. Augustine, FL, at my favorite time of day. This time of day changes in the blink of an eye. I'm happy to have captured it on film.

COCK, IAN ERIC

I am a soldier in the US Army. Photography is my hobby. I was stationed in the Republic of Panama for three years, and every day I ran by this one section with these flowers, and only a few at a time would bloom. I took the opportunity one day to snap a picture, and out it came.

COE, JESSICA

I took this picture when I was out to dinner for my birthday. I loved the way the clouds reflected in the water and had to take a picture of it! I hope to go to college for photography after graduation from high school.

COFFEY, JIM

This waterfall is made after a heavy rain. Water overflows from a large pond into a pasture, then it travels to a small creek bed where it finally reaches the edge of a road, and then it crosses it to form a waterfall known as "Dripping Springs." It is located between the small towns of Slidell and Leo, TX. My Aunt Sue, who married my dad's brother, Bernice Coffey, used to take showers here when she was a young girl. I am very glad I had the chance to take this picture because I know what this means to her.

COGSWELL, CHRISTOPHER

As I was driving around one fall day trying to capture the colors of the leaves changing, I ran across the road in this picture and noticed the great opportunity to test my photographic talent. I was amazed at how everything came together—from the colors of the leaves to the minor details of the tire tracks in the road. This is a picture that my family and I have thoroughly enjoyed.

COHAN, DONALD S.

This is a photo I took at a Better Living Center that had many displays and demonstrations. The little girl seemed so suspicious of this "con-man" with his shirt button popped open. I thought it was very humorous. Sometimes the real thing is funnier than something contrived.

COHEN, RALPH

This is a photograph taken from a balcony outside the revolving restaurant on the seventeenth floor of the Pier 66 Resort in Fort Lauderdale. The view looks northeast over the intracoastal waterway and the Atlantic Ocean. I have always lived near an ocean. Growing up in New York City, we spent summers at Rockaway Beach, and during college I was a lifeguard and R. B. I moved to south Florida in 1990, where you're never more than a thirty minute drive from the beach, which you can take advantage of all year round. I love to compose and shoot scenic photographs from unique perspectives.

COHEN, STEVEN D.

A physician by profession, I enjoy travel and photography. While on my honeymoon in Maui, I was trying out my new Nikon camera that my wife gave me as a wedding gift. How appropriate to see this bride and groom being photographed on the beach!

COLE, TAMMY

I believe photography was one of the most important inventions of time. To capture a single moment of our lives on film and share that memory always is a precious gift. This picture was taken on my son's birthday at the park. My 17-year-old daughter, Feliesha Ward, and her stepfather, Chad, were playing catch. Feliesha was so determined to at least try to catch each ball. A month after I entered this picture, Feliesha was killed in a car accident. But the many memories of her life caught on film will live on forever.

CONNELL, YVETTE DUMONT

"Sunset" was taken from our ninth floor living room window in Kingsbridge Heights, South Bronx, NY. We look over the Palisades across the Hudson River and are able to enjoy many hours of spectacular scenery, which I like to capture on camera. I enjoy making greeting cards for friends and relatives using my photography.

COOK, MARY

My mother and I were visiting family on the East Coast. When we stopped down at Cape Cod for the day, I realized I had one picture left on my film. I fell in love with this lighthouse. I have never taken such a great picture. I have shared reprints of this with my family and closest friends. Everyone enjoys it.

COON, MICHAEL JAMES

This is photo of my rottweiler, "Mickey." After I came home from work one day, he kept following me around. He looked so irresistible that I had to take his picture. I'm a social worker in West Virginia, but my dream is to make it as a photographer. I used to shoot strictly in black-and-white, but in the past two years I've begun shooting in color due to my changing tastes in photography. I feel that it's important to capture the emotion of the subject or to produce a lasting emotion in the person looking at my photos.

COPPER, PATRICIA

I have always enjoyed taking pictures of sunsets and nature. I have lived in my current house for five years, and I am still in awe of some of the scenes that I see from my backdoor. This "Majestic Moment" is one that I wanted to share with everyone, and what better way to share. I'm close to retirement and can hardly wait to spend more time taking more pictures of this view.

CORREA, YVONNE F.

In desert-like climates, the burst of a blooming spring flower is always so brief, as it is for this cactus flower. For only a few days a year, this beautiful spring cactus flower emerges with the morning sunlight and recedes with nightfall. Notice the shadow? They appear with the morning sun rising in the east. Note the shadow of a young tree that is not pictured in my photo. I am fascinated by the wonders of nature, people, animals, and only from afar, "The City Lights At Night." So you see, there is always a story to tell with photography, and for these reasons I continue to carry my camera.

CORRELL, JOYCE B.
Jarrod Mark, alias Sluggo, is my grandbaby. He definitely needs to do more crunches because at one hundred pounds, I can barely lift him, so what does a grandmother do? I watch and photograph him, attempting to catch those special moments.

CORSTANGE, BARBARA
Kyska, my wolf-hybrid, and I drove from Alaska to Massachusetts this past August. I came upon a nice area along Lake Superior to exercise her. She had such a good time playing in the water and running along the edge of the woods, experiencing new territory. Something caught her attention, I called her name, and snapped the picture. By no means am I a photographer, but I am proud of "On The Alert."

COUN, RACHEL
I see pictures everywhere, whether I am walking down a street or just staring out my apartment window. I am drawn to capturing color images where one doesn't expect to find them such as a rusty lock on a blue door in the East Village of New York City.

CRALEY, SUSAN E.
My husband, Mike, is taking Tanner, our grandson, to the Susquehanna River in Pennsylvania for his first fishing trip.

CRISELLE, LISA
A great subject for "people" photos is someone who, unknowingly, reveals a personal story through their facial expression. I met Mike from Minnesota during his beach-bum period in Key West. He'd just come from a physically exhausting venture working in an Alaskan fish cannery. I found him to be a fascinating subject, and it was difficult to choose one from the many successful shots.

CROOKE, SHUKURA K.
I took this picture one day while sitting on my back porch. The sun was shining so bright, and the sea was so calm. I could see the hills of St. Croix and Puerto Rico in the distance. Just watching over the water made me remember why I loved home—to experience days like this!

CROSS, CYNTHIA
I grew up in a small town in Barnwell, SC, which I loved very much and vowed to never leave. That was, by chance, when I fell in love with the sweetest man. He lived in Maryland, and to be closer to him I broke my vow and packed my bags. When there, I realized that Maryland, despite the crowded area, was incredible. It is full of beautiful mountains, seasons that you could see change before your eyes, and breathtaking farms. This particular farm is my favorite. One day when coming home from work, I drove by the farm. It had been raining but stopped and the sun was coming out. By chance I had my camera with me and took advantage of the situation. I hope this publishing is the first of many. I want photography to someday be my career, so I can catch that perfect moment in time and share it with others.

CROWELL, BETTY C.
Jennifer was our first grandchild. She was 17 months old and had flown with her parents from Columbus, OH, to spend Thanksgiving with her Vermont grandparents. She was such a joy to photograph, but this has always been one of our favorites. She was stepping out in our kitchen with our wonderful old cat, Smokey, who really didn't like children, as his displeasure expresses so well. Since this time, Jennifer has acquired two siblings, Christopher and Katie. I'm an amateur who doesn't usually enjoy taking pictures, but I wanted to capture these priceless expressions forever.

CUMMINGS, BETTY L.
I am not a photographer, nor even an amateur photographer, but I go around snapping whatever appeals to me. My husband and my mother adore one another. He had just finished giving her bedtime liquids and was waiting for me to help him get mother back to bed. When I came into the room and saw this, I thought it was precious and I said, "Hold that pose!" It seems to clearly express the tenderness and love between son-in-law and mother-in-law. My husband and I care for our mothers, who are both invalids, in our home.

CUMMINS, ELIZABETH
This photo was taken during a father-daughter moment that was so very special to the two of them. I looked out the window of the house at the sunset in our backyard, and not only did I see the beauty of a sunset, I also saw the beauty of love between a daddy and his little girl. Howard and Holly are so special to me that the moment captured on film made it more special.

CUNNINGHAM, TAMMY
I've always said that photography's in my veins. My dream and my goal is to become a professional photographer. Seeing one of my photographs published gives me such unspeakable joy. This picture is of my sister-in-law, Marsha, and her husband, Dave. I actually didn't think this picture would turn out so well, as I didn't have a flash. We were all pleased it did because out of all the pictures friends had taken, this was one of the few that came out at all. It was a beautiful wedding and truly "A New Beginning" of their life and everlasting love together.

CUSANO, MARLENE
At a memorial for deceased loved ones, a tree had the names of those who passed away on it, plus there was a release of balloons with the names in them. In trying to get a picture of the tree, the lower part of this lady's hair was included in the photo. It is very clear. I'm calling it her "Guardian Angel."

CZLAPINSKI, KATHRYN DYER
I am one of ten children. All of us are natural artists. My specialty is wall murals. Trompe L'oeil, baby décor, and hand-made stencils comprise only a part of my repertoire. I frequently utilize photography to get ideas for paintings. Thus, Christy and Paul, our instructors at the local Arthur Murray Dance Studio, posed for me. The grace and staccato sensuality of "The Tango Lesson" embodies motion in its most romantic guise. My husband, Larry, and I make our dance lesson a marvelous weekly date. It keeps the embers hot, hot, hot!

DABRITZ, BARBARA
This was my "dream come true" European vacation, which was further enriched by being with my family members who share my interests in European history. Our grand finale before leaving was this unscheduled stop at perhaps one of the most beautiful castles in England. Now, all I have to do is look at my photographs and I am once again transported back to all those magical moments in time.

DALTON, CAROLYN
The photograph of my grandson, Jeremy Schwab, was taken at my son's Ranch near San Angelo, TX. Jeremy was only 2½ years old and very intent on catching fish from one of the tanks on Uncle Greg's ranch. Jeremy lives in Austin, TX, with his mother, Holly, and visits frequently with his grandparents and uncle, who also reside in Austin. Photographing Jeremy and my three other grandchildren, Brittany, Bryan and Kennedy Marberry, is one of my greatest joys.

DANOFF, MILT
I never before have entered a photo contest. I am flabbergasted and ecstatic that my photo was selected for publication. I am 70, retired, and live in Santa Rosa, CA. I take lots of pictures in my travels. When I saw the ad for your contest in the newspaper, I thought why not try! I had just returned from a trip to France and was loaded with photos. I took this photo inside the beautiful and picturesque Mount Saint Michaels Monastery, which is a day's journey from Paris. The inside is now like a quaint village with many tiny shops along very narrow, steep, and winding walkways. I felt I had captured a natural charm and simplicity.

DARSEY, LAURA H.
With the wind bursting the clouds and the trees and moss swaying, this quite contented bloom eating up the sunshine at a kitchen in coastal Georgia smiles for one day, and then it is gone forever. When I look at it as it sits on the skyline, it brings to my mind God's plan for us: life for a little while here on earth, and then eternal life up there in heaven. I am a mother blessed with two wonderful boys, James Cody and Barrett Seth.

DAVIDSON, MARIE KADISHA
I'm a mother of three with a passion for photography—especially black-and-white. Although my usual subjects, Noah, Alexa, and Isaac, rarely volunteer a pose, I am able to capture some meaningful expressions from time to time. This particular one is of Alexa warning me to "Watch Out" after she had been playing in the hot Houston sun. My dream is to one day turn my passion into a living and give up working as a registered nurse in the ICU.

DE ROSA, ANTHONY
I've always had a love of taking pictures—still pictures or motion. I carry a camera to most of the affairs I attend and on every vacation. I took this picture in Nassau, Bahamas. It was a beautiful clear day, the clouds were starting to rise, the air and water seemed so restful and calm, and for the moment everything seemed so peaceful. I decided to shoot this scene from the sight-seeing tour

boat, on which I was touring the wonderful island scenery with my wife.

DECH, KENNETH

I found this baby kitten living back in the woods in the rocks three years ago. I would take food and milk back to him until I worked him up to eating in my yard. Since I found him living in the rocks, I named him Rocky. I live on a mountain where bears come to eat in my yard. The bears and I have our own special friendship. Rocky took up with a bear named Shanta, and they have united together. They would come to eat together and leave together as a unique pair. Both are still wild friends.

DERBENTLI, HILAL

I am an amateur photographer. I like taking spontaneous photographs, and that's why I carry my camera at all times. I took this photo because it represents tolerance to various religions. It is a photo of a place in Istanbul where a church and a mosque are located right next to each other.

DESTE, ERIK

When this picture was taken, I was in a very emotional state of mind. I loved it there, but I knew there was no chance of me staying. I took the last of my earnings, bought a disposable camera, and tried to capture the essence of what I enjoyed most about California. This picture was one of a few that I was the most pleased with. I am honored to have the opportunity to share it with everyone. I would like to say thanks to my family and to my true friends—you know who you are. I love you all.

DICKINSON, DON

I am a wanna-be farmer and I try to grow watermelons, so this time I planted sugar babies. They weren't very big, and my wife, who is a collector of porcelain dolls, thought it would be fun to picture one of her Indian dolls pushing a wheelbarrow with the big watermelons. We thought it was real cute that the doll made the watermelons look so big. He is so tiny that he looked like he couldn't handle them if they got any bigger. We took several pictures, but the one we submitted was the best.

DIXON, RHEA A.

My husband, Gary, and a couple of our friends like to spend our summer weekends riding our Harleys, looking for covered bridges and old mills. This is one we came across this summer. What a great escape from the city.

DRAGOO, BRINDA

My grandson wanted to be a girl for Halloween because he wanted to do something different. He is my pride and joy, and we do many things together when he comes to visit. He often stays the night and keeps in touch with us. I am an Avon repections and a home show cass seller. I keep busy as often as I can. I'm a mother of two daughters and three stepchildren, and I have two grandsons. I've lived in Portland for twenty-two years. My hobbies are knitting, reading, making good food, and more.

DRUMMOND, RAFFAELLA C.

My name is Raffaella Drummond. My husband, Robert, is a professional football player. Upon the birth of our son, my husband said to me, "Whether our baby is a boy or a girl, our child will be named after you." Hence, came the male version, *Rafael*. His name means "one who heals." Our son Rafael came into our lives at a very trying time. My husband had lost his father and I lost my grandmother in a period of one week. Our son eased our suffering with his never-ending smile and "Angelic Face."

DUCHENE, MAY

This is a photo of a statue of the Blessed Virgin Mary. She is the silent guardian at the garden cemetery. She watches over my husband, Jim's, grave. He passed away October 17, 1996.

DUELL, DOUGLAS L.

Being a former bull rider and having a love for the sport of rodeo led me to the idea of training Brahmas for show. This is my 7-year-old Brahma, Bandit; he'll steal your heart after a hot summer dog training session. We went to the shaded area, where I got him to lay and be brushed. After that, I layed upon him just to give him a hug. He sighed, I sighed, and the nap began. My wife, who had been taking pictures for me for our show book, took this one for me in disbelief. Coming to a fair or event near you: maybe Doug and Bandit.

DUKE, GERRI

I've worked in different art media, including graphic design, clay, wood sculpture, and tapestry. In recent years, I've focused on landscape oil paintings. But whether I have a paintbrush or camera in my hand, I'm inspired by natural environments, their diversity of forms, and the moods they evoke. In June 1999, when I photographed yoga teacher Pamela Asherah on a beach in Mexico, I was struck by the contrasts in moods and forms shown by her calm, meditative pose against breaking waves of the Sea of Cortez. "In The Moment" is a vision of peace in a turbulent world.

DUTRO, DEBBIE

This photo was taken on my first trip to Europe. A friend and I flew to Germany, rented a car, and spent a month driving. Aside from Germany, we visited Australia, Italy, France, and Switzerland. It was truly a once-in-a-lifetime experience for me. I went places and saw things I never thought I would have the opportunity to see: the canals of Venice, the Coliseum in Rome, the Leaning Tower of Pisa, Michelangelo's Statue of David, the Matterhorn, and the list goes on. Paris was the last stop before heading home to California. The Eiffel Tower was displaying "J-100 Avant L'an 2000," which means, "One hundred days until the year 2000."

EGGLESTON, ROBYN A.

This is a picture of my daughter, Alicia, last summer while at an archery tournament at the Crestmill Inn in Bedford, IN, with my husband, Rick, and my son, Sean. I had the camera aimed at the pool, and as I took the picture, Alicia splashed the water. I was very surprised at the coloration and shadows formed by the sunlight. As you can see, the shadows formed an image of a shark in the background. I think this is one of the best pictures I've ever taken.

ELLETT, MARGARET S.

My cat, Why Me, was asleep in a shallow basket on a table. I quietly sat in a nearby chair and took a series of pictures. As she awakened, it was tough deciding which shot to enter in this contest. My love of photography started as a young child when I began using a ninety-eight cent baby Brownie. When my children were small, I kept a loaded camera handy to take those special shots. Now as a senior citizen, photography is still a favorite hobby.

ELRICK, TAMMY

This photograph was taken on St. Simons Island, GA, at the United Methodist Conference Center, Epworth-By-The-Sea. As a summer camp counselor at Epworth, my counselor friends and I were stopped in our tracks by this view over the Frederica River as we led our young campers to the cabins after an evening program. Thankfully, I had my camera in tow as well. Nothing can recreate God's awesome creation, but I am glad that I was able to capture somewhat of a semblance. God proved His existence by this beautiful sunset better than we counselors ever could!

ELSENRAAT, LYDIA

I had just finished cleaning out the bottom of our washstand when our pekingese, Misty, crawled in. She really enjoyed it and had to be taken out. My husband suffers from Parkinsons, so he is mostly home-bound. Since I am his care-giver, I am home most of the time. So, our little dog is very special to us and is our constant companion.

EMANUELLI, JOHN

How resplendent! We were two Floridians at last in Alaska—the "Greatland," the "Last Frontier." This was to be our first campsite, at Granite Creek, amidst the creek bed, fireweed, and cascading mountain backdrop with low-hung misty clouds as if in a dream. We were drinking it up, each with our own viewfinder—my wife, Joy, with binoculars, and I with camera lens. This pristine view will forever be framed in our mind's eye as our trip's first memory, our "Alaska Reverie."

ERGUIAGA, WYNARDA

This photo is of our beautiful niece Renae and her brand new husband, Kelly, at their wedding reception last fall. Whatever Kelly told Renae, it must have been really good. To me this picture indicates what their marriage is going to be like—priceless!

ESPINOSA, L. G.

This was an action shot. The bride was not posing for this shot. It looks like it was taken back in the 1930s, but I took it on October 16, 1999. I did not use any special effects to capture the moment.

EVANS, SUSAN

I have always been drawn to photography of the natural world. As a park ranger, I have been fortunate to work in several powerful and picturesque places. The funny thing about this photo is that it was taken in a hurry. I was setting up for the shot when I heard a loud group of boy scouts running down the trail. Not wanting the ruckus to spoil the peace and tranquillity I felt in the grotto, I quickly set up and took the shot. It just goes to show that Mother Nature is indeed the true artist.

EVRETT, BRIAN
The Orioles had been nesting in my yard for three consecutive years. In the spring of 1999, two chicks had apparently fallen from the nest prematurely. I heard them chirping for quite some time and noticed that they could not yet fly. Knowing there are cats in the area roaming freely, I wanted to help them. Using a stick as a perch, I helped them to safety. After watching the mother do several feedings, I was able to get this beautiful shot of nature in action.

FAULKNER-YOUNGREN, KATHY
When I went to Egypt, my favorite monument was the Great Sphinx. Our Teton is stately and awe-inspiring like this statue. Here, he holds a grape as he poses on Mom's Egyptian carpet. He has impeccable taste for the finest things in life. He is athletic, as well as refined, and runs either with Mom, my brother Scott, or with me. My husband and I run ultra-races over 26.2 miles all over the United States, and although Teton cannot run races with us, he can train with us. Indeed, Teton is versatile and intelligent—exceptional in every way!

FEDAK, TERESA
I enjoy taking pictures of our dogs. This is Sugar, our chocolate Labrador retriever with her first litter of puppies at 1 day old. We raised Sugar from our first litter, so she is our "baby." That made her first litter extra special. She is a wonderful mother, and this photo captures that essence. My hobbies include collecting and showing model horse statues and gardening. I love anything involving animals and nature. I grew up in the suburbs of Chicago, IL, and moved to Colorado in 1998. I enjoy driving in the mountains and photographing the spectacular views and wildlife.

FERGUSON, DAVID
This is a photo of my daughter, Amber, riding Prince Charles in her first year of competition. I took a lot of pictures that day, but I thought the look of concentration on her face as the two jumped this vertical as one made a good picture. Amber was 13 at the time. Prince Charles, or Charlie, was 19, and he retired after this show.

FINNIGAN, HEATHER
I am a 58-year-old Nana who hails from Scotland. I love children and animals. I helped in a private day care and took photos of the children so their parents could see the smiles they were missing because they had to work. Unfortunately, my grandchildren moved further away and I no longer work at the day care. I was left with such a void. I then decided to capture on film my son's lizards and every amphibian, insect, and rodent with whom I feel a connection and compassion for. As they say, a picture is worth more than a thousand words.

FIRTH, DOLORES
I love taking pictures anywhere, everywhere, and of whoever. I like especially taking quick "shots of the moment" that are memorable and different. My first memorable gift was a camera. I have baskets throughout my home filled with photos that I change out from time to time. When our family has get-togethers, we often look through these baskets, and they are treasured moments in themselves. This photo is special to me because it is the exact moment of the dawn of a new day, wondrous and different from the one before and the one after.

FLOWERS, SARAH L.
This little angel came to us by way of kitty purgatory on his way to kitty heaven. He captured our hearts with his bright blue eyes and delighted our souls with his light. He left us as quickly as he had come; quietly in my arms he passed away while tearing out a piece of my heart. It was a great honor that he chose to share what little time he had with us. He will live in our hearts for eternity; and now, thanks to this publication, he will visit homes across the nation. We were truly blessed.

FOCA, GALE L.
Gale is a nurse who enjoys nature photography; she finds nature healing. This picture was taken while visiting Maine with her son, Brian. Brian is also an avid photographer and tends to snap a wider range of photos, including architecture, people, and nature.

FORD-ANDERSON, CARLA
We have two cocker spaniels, Ashante and Domino, and two cats, Felix and Queen of Sheba. I love taking pictures of them when they are just being. This posed photo was at the insistence of our daughter, Samantha, who had just dressed Ashante up in her Santa hat and needed to preserve this moment for posterity. I never imagined that Ashante would become a celebrity and I would actually be called an "amateur photographer."

FOSDAL, MARIAN
This photograph was taken during a medical missions trip in South America. I could not pass up the opportunity to take a picture of the friendly child who had come to bathe along the shore of the Amazon River close to where our riverboat had stopped. The child lived in one of the pueblos we visited near Iquitos in northeastern Peru.

FREE, ANN
This is a photo of my baby, Tammy. She has had a long day! She plays with a small football in a sock. After dinner she takes a nap in her bed. I'm retired, so I take lots of pictures of her. She loves to chase the squirrels.

FRIZZELL, TODDI
The evening I saw this marvelous sky of clouds with shafts of light piercing though, I wanted to take several pictures of it. I'm totally an amateur photographer. I use disposable cameras; they're great for me. I love to take pictures and work them into personal mailings. It is so wonderful to be able to have your own personal, individual touches when writing or giving gifts. Others seem to appreciate and enjoy it when they're on the receiving end. It is a great honor to me to have "Evening's Eve" in *Eye Of The Beholder*.

FULTON, SHEILA L.
The dog is Clyde, a 150 pound Great Pyrenees, and his buddy is Howard, a two pound Siamese cross. The "odd couple" are inseparable.

GARCIA, LORI Q.
This is a photo of our son, Chase, on his first Halloween. Chase's nickname is Honey Bee, so it seemed appropriate for him to be just that. His pal, Winnie the Pooh, was dressed to match. Chase may have been dressed like a bumble bee, but to us he is our little angel. We are truly blessed to have this incredible little boy in our lives. We love little Honey Bee!

GARRISON, LAURA
Color is a very important element of my photography. The morning glory pool at Yellowstone National Park is a vivid subject to photograph. I waited until the clouds parted for the light to be just right for this shot. It was worth the wait.

GASTON, FAYE
My grandson, Bryan Rodopoulos, is serious about "asking the blessing" before meals. He is only 2 years old but has the spotlight with his memorized prayer that is a song. This photo was not planned but is a genuine moment in a fast-food restaurant. I am an amateur photographer in a small town. My favorite photos are of my four grandchildren, but I make photographs of community events as a volunteer to save bits of history. Many are published in our local weekly newspaper. Many ladies here share their recipes. I share my photographs.

GEORGE, PAULETTE
Hi, I am Kaitlyn, an adopted and retired therapy dog. I previously worked primarily with depressed and troubled youth and adults. I also visited school classrooms as a lesson. I enjoy adults, children, and babies. I kiss them all! For relaxation, my companion person, Paulette, and I both enjoy the New Jersey shore, Pennsylvania's mountains, and taking pictures. I really enjoy posing as a hobby. I guess I'm just a ham of a dog!

GERAW, JANICE
I had been out on Enosburg's back roads, taking photos of the brilliantly beautiful foliage on this autumn day when on my way home, I met this cow coming right at me. I stopped the car because you just don't know what a cow is going to do. Not daring to get out of my car because she was going full speed, I took this photo through the windshield. Cows are not often known to run. Luckily, I had my camera at hand.

GIBBENS, CURTIS A.
I worked in southeast Alaska for four months. I took advantage of the location on weekends and came back with many pictures of beautiful mountains, eagles, and whales. Since I have returned to Virginia, I have learned much more about photography through John Shaw's books and tapes, and I also attended his workshop. Now I really would like to go back up and find another "Tail Of A Whale."

GIBSON, VIRGINIA
Mr. Burnett turned 99 on the ninth day of the ninth month of 1999. His birthday was celebrated on television because of all the nines. He had pictures in the newspaper and was surrounded by loving family and friends. I lovingly call him Dad because his three children live elsewhere. I call him every day to check on him. He is a very godly man. His mind is still sharp. He's my friend. We've been friends for over fifty years.

His son Roy and I were high school sweethearts. We are all best friends.

GILSON, PATRICIA
A very dear grandchild, Jazzy, who is 3 years old, loves my dog, Happy Dawg. I just happened to have the camera handy when they were playing. There is just something so captivating about children and animals together—it's love in it's purest form.

GIMBEL, CONNIE
I have always enjoyed the extraordinary sights that nature provides. My favorites are those seen in clouds, rainbows, and sunsets. I enjoy capturing the beauty of nature that is only visible for a short interlude in time so others can also enjoy the beauty I have seen. This photo was taken from my front yard just as a stormy day was coming to an end. My youngest son, who is the artistic one in the family, has been encouraging my interest in photography along with help from my fiance and oldest son.

GLASEN, JULIE
This picture was taken one summer evening on the commercial fishing vessel *Morning Thunder,* near Cordova, AK. *Morning Thunder* belongs to my father, Mike Glasen, and holds nine years of some of the most memorable moments of my life.

GOODMAN, WILLIAM A.
I am a part-time photographer that tries to catch some beautiful things God created so that others may see. I started out trying to learning how to draw at 9 years old and have since changed to drawing with a camera.

GRAHAM, ANTHONY
This image was taken while on a thirteen mile ride through Red Rock Canyon, which is about twenty-five minutes outside of Las Vegas, NV. This particular area reminds me of my wife and I on our twenty-third wedding anniversary in Hawaii, with black sand beaches and red rock mountains gleaming from afar. Traveling and taking beautiful pictures is worth taking up as a hobby.

GRAY, ALFRED W.
Chateau Azay-Le-Rideau is located in the lovely Loire Valley, southwest of Paris. The original castle met disaster in 1418, when Charles VII was the Dauphin and was insulted by the Burgundian Guard as he passed through Azay. Charles caused the town to be seized and burned and the whole guard, a captain and 350 soldiers, were summarily executed. It wasn't until 1527 that the chateau was rebuilt in its present form and appearance. It was then purchased by the French State in 1905, and is now open to tourists throughout the year.

GRELOCH, PAT
My husband, Tony, and I put a ceramic rabbit with a basket at our front door for Easter. We put Easter straw and plastic eggs in the basket. Two days after Easter, a robin started removing the Easter straw and all but one plastic egg. She then started making her nest and layed three eggs. They hatched one at a time. Our grandchildren, D.J., age 6, and Erika, age 4, were so thrilled with

watching each day as nature developed. It was such a beautiful learning experience for all of us.

GROSSMAN, JEFF
Mythology and legend reside not only in our imaginations, but through our lenses. Having visited Greece to assimilate the magical history and mythological background, I was enchanted one morning by a fisherman off the island of Crete who slowly paddled his craft before me. Perhaps it was the incarnation of the boatman of the River Styx transporting us into another place at another time. In that captured instant lives a thousand tales. Using photography, I seek to provoke stories rather than tell them. I graduated from University at Albany in 1995, with a BA in film as dramatic art. My family members are Robert, Linda, Debbie, Mike, and Michael.

GRZESKOWICZ, LINDA
While playing with Phoebe one morning, I set my camera on a tripod, watched her through the viewfinder, and patiently waited in hopes of getting a picture of her suitable for framing. I wanted to capture her kittenhood on film. Phoebe came through for me when she stood up on her hind paws, hung on to the bicycle handlebar, and started biting it. I snapped the picture. I've always enjoyed taking pictures; however, in the past few years my interest in photography has grown. I also enjoy the outdoors and hiking.

GUNTHER, RICHARD
This is my most treasured photo of the happiness of those two together. They always went everywhere together. Since this photo was taken, our boxer, Poncho, has since passed away, and our loving little Peppie has all those loving memories of him. We love them both, and this picture has so much meaning to the whole family. We will always treasure the time we have had with our best friends and companions.

GWIN, PAM
My husband and I were staying in Chicago while he was attending a medical meeting. My kids, Jason and Missy Smith, wanted a photo of the skyline of Chicago. My nephew, Kyle, took us to see the "Fountain," so I took my tripod and camera and started shooting. I was lucky in getting this shot. I take pictures all of the time, but it is all guesswork. I am a part-time CPR instructor who loves teaching. I do stained glass for a hobby. I am totally hooked on HGTV and the Discovery Channel.

HALL, CHERYL C.
This photo was taken by me on Halloween. It's of my 4-year-old brother, Kyle. Their mother makes their costumes and likes original costumes. They are grandma's pride and joy. They are more clowns than bums.

HALL, FRIEDA M.
I was visiting my daughter in Florida, and my 20-month-old granddaughter was watching her mother putting on her makeup when she leaned over and picked up the eye-lash curler and tried to curl hers. It turned out better than I expected, seeing how small the bathroom in that trailer was.

HALL, MARY C.
My husband bought me a new camera, and a friend gave us tickets to the Alabama football game. This is my favorite picture from the four rolls of film I used. It was a perfect day; we won.

HALL, SHARON
This is a picture of my little girl, Paige, on a beautiful October afternoon, and although I take many pictures of her, this one holds a special place in the hearts of me and her daddy. When you capture the look of innocence on a child's face, you know you've done something magical, and I wanted to share that with everyone. I hope you enjoy it as much as we do.

HAMAKER, DANIELLE
First off, I wish to introduce you to the model in this picture. Her name is Magic K. At the time when this photo was taken, we just adopted her and didn't know of her many talents. As you can see, she loves getting her picture taken. Every time we take out the camera, she starts getting ready, and then proceeds into posing. We have other great poses, but this is our favorite. Hope you enjoy this photo of our "Marilyn" as much as we do.

HAMILTON, KROSS
This was Kross' first time to go trick-or-treating. When we got the picture back, we realized his mouth and face expressions were the same as the picture of tigger on his outfit. After the first door he was a professional trick-or-treater: knock on the door, say trick-or-treat, thank you, and to his amazement—candy!

HANSEN, TERRI A.
This was taken over twenty years ago with a plain household camera. It was at Port Aransas, TX, while on vacation. My son (right) and a friend's daughter were fishing. We had only one pole and one sun hat for the two of them. We told them they would have to take turns with each.

HANSHAW, BONITA
This photograph was taken at the zoo last summer. It reminded me of lovers having a spat. In 1985, an eye disease rendered me legally blind. As a result, my picture taking is often a hit and miss process. Therefore, when the perfect picture is taken, it makes me very happy. At the zoo, some of the animals were too far away for me to see very well. I zoomed in on them in the hopes that a beautiful picture would result. Then I had to wait until the pictures were developed to see my memories.

HARBOUR, MARGARET
This picture was taken at the Japanese Gardens in Fort Worth, TX. I really did not think the photo would take, as the sun was so bright. I love to take pictures of family and places we visit. When I thought about what I would put in this profile, I looked at the picture to remember the moment it was taken. The thing it brought most to mind was someone who loved taking pictures as much as I, so this one's for you, Gary. We love and miss you.

HARDESTY, STEPHEN
I was out taking pictures one early morning in October at a lake on the outskirts of town, and not

much was happening when this duck landed. I had to belly crawl with my camera and 300mm lens within about five feet to get this great picture. I enjoy taking pictures of all kids of things, from people, to wildlife, to buildings. It is a real thrill to capture a picture as unique as this one.

HARRIS, JANET
We were in the rugged wilderness of South Dakota's Bad Lands when I took this photo. We were amazed at how the pioneers of olden times crossed this vast, rugged wilderness. This was just one of the many places we visited on a cross-country trip last summer. Since we are retired, we love to travel and see the USA. We enjoy taking videos and photos of where we go and what we see and then enjoy sharing them with family and friends.

HARTER, ADRIENNE M.
Driving home a few months after Hurricane Andrew "visited" south Florida, I nonchalantly looked over at a pile of debris, which was commonplace due to massive clean-up efforts. A small sunflower peeked out. How uplifting it was to see such a beautiful work of nature that had survived the storm! It was growing and thriving amongst a state of chaos and ugliness. I felt better than I had in months. To this day, eight years later, sunflowers still inspire me. They remind me that no matter what happens, goodness and beauty will always find a way to shine through.

HATTER-TAYLOR, ROBIN
This is a special picture of my Arabian gelding and my uncle's black lab. I am always trying to take a picture that captures the different personalities that animals have. I really think that when you look at a picture, you can see a story. I am a full-time mother of two, and I enjoy taking pictures of my animals and my family.

HAUTER, CAROLYN SUE
"Beautiful Bride" is a photograph of a friend's daughter. I had taken pictures at Lindsay's wedding to help cut her expenses. I enjoy taking pictures at weddings of family and friends. I also enjoy taking photos of sunsets, sunrises, and flowers, and while I travel. I have taken pictures for years and entered some in small county fair contests, and when my cousin, Jacki, encouraged me to enter a picture in this contest, I figured I had nothing to lose.

HEARN, AMY
I am a graduate teaching assistant at Virginia Commonwealth University in Richmond, VA. I have many animals and frequently take abused and neglected animals of all breeds, sizes, and ages. I first discovered Whiskey in 1996. He was 3 years old when I received him. Prior to being rescued, Whiskey suffered from extreme abuse and neglect. Despite the repercussions of his past, he fully embraced love and affection from human beings. Within months, he completely gained faith and trust in me as his friend. To this day, he amazes me with his unique character and his grateful heart. Whiskey is happy, playful, and flamboyant. I ride, interact with him, and take his picture so often that he decided to add something "extra" on this day! I couldn't ask for a better horse.

HEATH, ROBERT
We call these two our "kids." Calie will soon be 13 years old, while Joe was given to my husband just prior to Christmas 1998 by his son and now is about 1fi years old. They both keep us amused in their own ways. It seems so strange to hear a bird say phrases like "Kitty, Kitty, Kitty," "Calie, Calie, Calie," "Calie Kitty cat," "Calie outside," "Calie in house," "Hi Joe," "Good Morning Joe," or "Come Here." Calie is not aggressive, but at the same time, we don't trust the cat. There are times while we are gone that they are both left alone in the house, but of course Joe is safely in his cage. And when we travel in our fifth wheel, they both go with us; and while we are sightseeing and visiting, they are left in the trailer.

HECHLER, JANICE L.
I am a naturalist and believe there is beauty in all that surrounds us. "Urban Sunrise," which was taken at the hazardous waste dumpsite in Columbus, OH, proves it!

HECKLER, DEBRA J.
This is a photo of my dog, Duchess. I had the money laying on the table, and she picked it up and ran under another table. It took a lot for me to get the money without tearing it apart.

HERMSEN, MICHELE
It's here! It was a day we will never forget, and I am still in shock. At 8:00 P.M. we got a call from Dr. Kichuck: "Mrs. Hermsen, we have a donor heart for your son." That is all I heard; my precious boy is getting his chance, and his new heart would be transplanted that evening. Matt and I sat by Josh's bedside and prayed. We told him not to be scared but to be excited. He had been given one last chance. At 12:20 A.M. on August 18, the doctors rolled Josh into the operating room. We kissed him goodbye, until tomorrow.

HICKMAN, DIANNE
This photo was taken at a romantic spot my husband, Shane, and I found while we were still dating. Located in southeast Oklahoma, it's somewhat of a drive for us, but well worth it. I feel this picture captures part of the beautiful scenery and relaxing sensation that we love about this special place.

HIGDON, JUNE T.
The morning I took the photograph, "Autumn Sunrise," my daughter called me while on her way to work so I would see the beautiful sunrise. I went to the door, saw the sky, and reached for my camera. I thought, "This is a scene worth preserving because never again will it occur quite the same." My husband, Leonard, and I have four children, seven grandchildren, and four great-grandchildren living within a twenty mile radius of our home. We enjoy traveling but are always happy to return to our home in beautiful Pleasant Valley, MD, which lies between the Blue Ridge Mountains to the east and Elk Ridge to the west.

HODGE, VALERIE
It all started on April 13, 1994, when this little ball of soft white fur entered my world. Since that time, Krystle has been my constant companion and frequent subject of my camera lens. As a result of her sparkling personality and love of all mankind, it was only natural for her to become a certified pet therapy dog. Krystle's gentle, playful ways have put smiles on the faces of countless chronic and terminally ill children, and she has touched the hearts and licked the faces of so many needy people. Krystle is my world! She is my best friend.

HODGES, MARTHA
I never take a trip, short or long, by car or airplane, that I don't take my camera. You never know where or when you will find the perfect picture. This photo was taken on a car trip to Las Vegas. I was amazed at the difference between the size and shape of these two cactus growing side by side. It looks as though they were planted this way, but they were grown natural in the middle of the desert. My hobbies include photography, reading, puzzles, traveling, and family. My husband and I have one grown son.

HOLMS, BRUCE A.
This photo of Dorothy Lake was the best of four rolls of photos taken during a weekend backpacking trip. Each morning, the water was so still that it formed an almost perfect mirror of the surrounding mountains and contrasting, rust-colored loose rock. Dorothy Lake is located at an altitude of 10,000 feet in the Sierras south of Mammoth Lakes, CA, and is a worthwhile moderate day-hike from Convict Lake for those inclined to visit. Mr. Holms is employed as a senior engineer at a Southern California aerospace company and is a 1988 graduate of the University of Florida.

HOLZINGER, JAMES
I was born Feb 14, 1937, and have been a plumber for forty years. "Day's End" was taken from the third floor balcony of the condo where my wife, Barbara, and I live. It overlooks the river. One of the reasons we moved here is because of the beautiful sunsets. I'm still working and have found many a night of tranquility and peace of mind after a long day.

HOPKINS, DAN
This is a photo of my dog, Shayna, which means "beautiful." She is a black and tan coonhound and is 10 years old. My idea for naming "The Lookout" was quite simple; it is the way I feel about my dog. She's always looking out for me. I took this photo at the ranch we used to own. By taking pictures of those dear to us, we create a "forever" memory. One of the happiest days of my life was bringing her home from the Humane Society. Adopt a shelter dog. They truly are man's best friend.

HORSWILL, C. WEIR
Christmas is always a beautiful day, but some are more beautiful than others. In 1998, for two days our community experienced a heavy ice storm. Early Christmas morning, the sun reappeared. The bright morning light turned on nature's own miniature Christmas lights in the ice covering all the trees and branches, each blade of grass, and even the telephone lines. It was a most beautiful Christmas morning.

HORTON, LAUREL
This picture was taken on one of our "Girl" week-

ends to a little cabin in Peru, VT. These are three of my closest friends, Cathi, Jane and Patti, who have come to accept my frequent picture taking and have become (usually) willing subjects. The creek where this was taken runs alongside the cabin, and we spend many hours hiking and exploring the region. I am a picture nut and have been known to take several rolls in a single weekend.

HOWALD, EDWIN W.
This photo is of a redtail hawk that made no move to leave its dinner. I walked as close as I dared and took three pictures from different angles. Its posture was saying, "Go find your own dinner." I retired from pionetics where I was a subcontractor to the Department of Defense in St. Louis, MO, April 1, 1987. After my wife of fifty years died in 1992, I moved to Hilton Head Island, SC. I've photographed sunsets, flowers, people, birds, deer, and other animals in South Carolina. I have always had a camera since my teen years. It was my first love and has kept me young.

HOWAT, LOIS
I am a very proud and grateful grandmother who has taken thousands of pictures that are mostly out of focus or over-exposed. However, I finally got it all together with a little luck to capture the best photo I ever took of my granddaughter, Peyton, when I took her to Six Flags Great Adventure this past fall for "Family Night," which happened to coincide with Peyton's third birthday. I truly believe that this picture captures the excitement and joy that Peyton was experiencing at that second. I will be able to relive that moment forever by simply looking at the picture and seeing the thrill of the experience each time in Peyton's face, which is now frozen in time forever.

HRANAC, MICHAEL
I am a true "amateur" photographer. Lester is a real miracle. He survived a run-in with a car and, with the help of dedicated doctors, is almost back to his adorable self. He used up several of his "lives" but continues to grace the rooms of our home in Boise, ID. I will continue to snap photos of interesting activities whenever the opportunity presents itself.

HUNT, GENE
I have been interested in photography for many years, and am just now getting around to pursuing it. I enjoy taking action photographs such as this one. "Pelican" was taken while my family and I were vacationing in Cocoa Beach, FL. It was one of those instances where you only have one chance to snap the photo, and I was lucky to do so.

HUSTON, REBECCA M.
This is a photo of my daughter, Madison, on a very hot summer day in 1999. Madison is about 15 months old here, and we are over at Grandpa's house. Even without her little pool, she still managed to find some water to play in. I was so glad to have my camera with me, because when I turned around and saw her, it was too cute. I knew not to chase her out, let alone say anything to ruin this moment. This picture makes me laugh every time I look at this precious little girl just having fun.

HUTCHINS, ELIZABETH M.
My husband, Floyd, and I were flying back to Fountain, CO, after visiting relatives in the Seattle area. Soon the pilot said Mount Rainer could be seen on our left, where we were seated. I reached for my bag, got my camera out, and took several pictures. This was such a unique view of Mount Rainer from the air. We have four children: Alan and Kelvin Hutchins, Amelia Carrillo, and Kathryn Czanderna. We also have three granddaughters: Verta and Colette Hinckley, and Ashley Hutchins, who we lost at an early age. I was born and raised in Charles City, IA, where I graduated from high school in 1945. I have been in taking pictures since I purchased my first camera in 1948. Besides taking pictures, I love to read, crochet, sew, quilt, and embroider, and I do crossword puzzles and put pictures puzzles together whenever I can. I would say if you like to take pictures, do it every chance you get whether flying, riding in a car, or even at home, indoors or outside.

HUTCHINSON, MARTHA C.
My husband, John, and I live in the Ocala National Forest. Besides taking pictures of our Kitty, we take pictures of deer, wild turkeys, and sand hill cranes. We love our retirement here.

ILSLEY, JIM
It has been said that one picture is worth a thousand words. There is certainly no mistake that April Evangeline is very sure Santa is on the phone. When my Aunt Lena received her Christmas card, she called us. She was very excited and felt like we should enter it in a contest.

JACKOBOICE, EDWARD M.
The awe-inspiring sight of Iguazu Falls is half of the picture; the sound of roaring waters is awesome too! You feel the spray, mist, and jungle humidity at the national boundaries of Paraguay, Brazil, and Argentina. While in South America for seven years as a Christian missionary, I enjoyed occasional opportunities to photograph God's creation and am happy to share this special place with you.

JAY, ROSEMARY
Sunsets are a passion with me. When traveling or on a family vacation, I always try to take a sunset picture. "Serenity" was taken on a family vacation at Torch Lake, MI, in August 1999. It is interesting to document the beauty of nature so others can enjoy it.

JESSEN, ROBERT
This is Dustin Hennessey, our great-grandson, at 18 months; he now is 4 years old. His mom and dad take him fishing and camping, and they teach him to be a good stewart of the earth, land, water, air, and all of God's animals. My wife, Donna, and I are retired. We raised three boys and taught them to respect all living things that God has created.

JOHNSON, JUDY
A distance of fifteen thousand miles separates me from my first grandchild, so pictures are of extreme importance. This is Noah using his new swing, which he received for his first birthday. From grampa, he loves to have to have his picture taken and, at times, can really "ham" it up.

JOHNSON, LARISA
While wandering around my grandparent's farm in Minnesota, I paused to look at how two seemingly different items came together to make such a unique and beautiful scene. I took this picture to remind people that our personal differences can work together; we can supplement each other to create a beautiful life and world. Differences should help us recognize the wonder of life and of each other and not create unfounded animosity.

JOHNSON, MELLANY J.
The photo was taken at Rockhound Park in New Mexico. I've never thought of myself as a photographer, but after looking through my photos, family members realized this one picture had a uniqueness about it. The lizard had actually stood there and dared me to click the shutter. When on vacation, my family and I are always keeping our eyes peeled for the strange and different. All I can say is that for once I was in the right place, at the right time, with the right equipment—a camera. Thank you, Mom and Dad, for the chance at success.

JOHNSON, B. K.
When I took this picture, I was a first class pilot for the ports of Long Beach and Los Angeles Harbors, CA. This picture is one of the long beach pilot boats that transports the pilots to and from ships arriving and departing the ports. This picture was taken at the Long Beach pilot station looking towards Palos Verdes, PA.

JONES, JUNE
I am a nurse and have dealt with sickness and death for more than thirty years. My release comes from camping and hiking with my dog, Cocoa, to places where I feel total happiness and closeness with God. My "Captured Aura" reflects my love for nature. This is a self-portrait taken with a timer on my camera.

JORDAN, ROSA
She is the daughter of Mr. Cornell Stigger and "mother," Almedia Stigger. Kirirsten Nicole is a very beautiful little girl. When I take a picture of her, it is as though she knows what I am looking for. She can make any photo look good. She is only 2 years old and loves to take pictures.

JOYE, GARY F.
This photo was taken in Saltillo, Mexico, when I was travelling with a group of missionaries. While passing through Saltillo, we decided to go shopping. The accordion player is blind and a regular fixture in the shopping square. I have taken three trips to Mexico, and he has always been playing on the street. This image has become symbolic of our church's mission in Mexico. My interest in photographs of people began with my involvement with missionary work in Mexico. It was a good move.

JUSTICE, BARBARA
It was a beautiful October day. My best friend, Jaunita, and I went for a ride to the Breaks Interstate Park for a picnic. The park is most beautiful in October, when the leaves are changing color and the winds are calm. We walked for a while and then we went to Laurel Lake, where I

took this picture that captured the peace and beauty of the day.

KACHEL, MURRY M.

It was a tender moment. Sister, Lauren Clark, holds her 4-month-old baby brother, Madison Murry Kachel. This picture was taken with my new Kodak DC200 Mega Pixel camera with a 864 by 152 resolution. Mom, Faith, and older sister, Elizabeth, think this is probably the best photo of Lauren lately, and Madison looks like he has something devious in mind. I sure love them all. I take pictures whenever I can, since the digital camera offers no more running into town to get a roll developed. There are many beautiful scenes at my Ranchito.

KAKACEK, RUTH E.

I paint in oil and acrylic. I was born November 20, 1926, in Otho, IA. Soon my parents moved to Pilot Mound on a farm. A memory I have of my dad picking me up is him putting me in a horse and buggy and going to Pilot Mound to see if the bank was really closed in 1929. When I was 7 years old we moved up Back Bone Hill into Bone County on a farm surrounded by timber and a beautiful orchard. Here I learned to love the trees and the wildlife. I've used a camera since I was 16 years old. Coming home from Iowa City, I stopped at Steam Boat Rock to take pictures. I took this picture of the falls on the Iowa river in the fall of 1999.

KARAHODA, JETON

The guitar shown in the photo is one of the guitars that Pete Towsant of the band "The Who" broke on the stage, and it is displayed now in the lobby of the "Rolling Stone Magazine" office. The picture was taken one night while I was working there as a night guard, and is a self portrait. Since I was playing guitar in a band in my youth, that night I couldn't resist not to marry my passion in music in the past with my passion for photography in the present and in the future. I am a medical doctor, and I have been working odd jobs since I came to the U.S. I was born in Prishtina, Kosova, where many dreams have been broken, but my philosophy is keep dreaming until one day you find your true voice.

KILLILEA, JACQUELINE

My late husband would be so proud of me again. I am still capturing that special moment. I was recently a first place winner in a local contest with a photo of my late husband, Paul, and my grandson Ryan putting on their makeup when dressed as clowns. I am constantly taking photos, and I utilized this interest on our Caribbean vacation in Aruba. Recently, I had my camera next to me when this iguana climbed up this jug to look inside curiously. I was thrilled with my capture and thrilled at being there at the right time.

KING, DEAN C.

This photo was taken on the campus of the University of Colorado at Boulder. At the time I took the photo, there was scarcely anything moving in the area, and I thought it was a good representation of a lazy summer afternoon. I like to take pictures of quiet scenes that cause the viewer to reflect on simpler things. Although I have lived in urban areas for a num-

ber of years, I am originally from a rural area in South Dakota and like to use picture settings that suggest a quiet, reflective lifestyle.

KIPLINGER, KATHY J.

The Christmas of 1998, I received my first 35mm camera. From that moment on I started to see things in a new light. There are so many beautiful things in this world that most people don't even notice—like this sunset I caught at one of my favorite places to sit and watch the sky. Sunsets are my favorite things to photograph, along with landscapes and trees. My idea behind my pictures is to show people all the beauty around them that passes by unnoticed. I hope to someday begin to sell my own work and ultimately put together books.

KIRBY, FRANCES K.

This photo of a dad and daughter at Coolidge Water Park in Chattanooga, TN, was taken of my son, David, and my granddaughter, Danielle, at night by the water fountain with their reflections in the water and the lights of the walking bridge in the background. Their image and reflections in the water captured a special moment for them.

KITTEN, JANET

This is a photo of my 7-year-old daughter, Lana, and her dog, Buddy. Buddy is always by Lana's side when she pays in the backyard. But on this day, Lena made sure Buddy wasn't going to leave her side at all. It was a hot day when this picture was taken. I had sprinkled the sand with water to make it cooler. Apparently, Lana figured Buddy needed to cool off too! I always like to take pictures of my kids. So, I always have a loaded camera on hand. This picture was so cute. I can't believe Buddy actually stayed still for so long.

KLINTS, LOU ELLEN

I waited many years to see my family grow, marry, and be out on their own. Now at this point in my life, never in my wildest dreams did I ever expect to have competition using the bathroom at four in the morning. Boy, was I wrong!

KNAPCZYK, KATHY

Baby Bear was born with a disability, a cleft palate, and she's had four surgeries to fix the problem. She is very spoiled and hand raised by me. She outgrew her bed, so I gave her one of my pillows. When she's napping with her toys (she has fifty-seven toys), do not touch them, or she gets upset! Then I call her grumpy. She is very friendly and loves everybody. We call her the Miracle Puppy.

KNOWLES, WILLIAM

This is not sibling rivalry, but the love and reuniting of a brother and a sister in the backwoods of Maine after a long winter apart. Abby and Boomer are getting re-acquainted and are out for a frolic. They are neighbors during the summer and fall months but are miles apart during the winter months. So, they are happy once again to be together. I am delighted with the results of this "lucky" shot!

KOCZUR, WANDA J.

This is a photo of my one and only grandchild, Nicholas. He was born the day before my birth-

day, and he means the world to me. It was a very hot and humid day, so my daughter took off his swim diaper. As he stood there so still, I just could not resist that cute little butt. I had to take a picture.

KOENIG, CAROL

I couldn't pass this picture up. Willie always slept in odd positions. One time he was on Tex, our boxer's, back. I had no film for that picture. I waited for my chance, and, "Bam," there it was—Willie making himself at home. He slept there for about a half hour. Willie can do anything to Tex and it won't bother him. It seems odd, but Willie is the proctor of Tex.

KONCHER, BARBIE

This is Max, our beloved family pet. The picture was taken in Arlington, VA, and was Max's first experience with snow. He wasn't sure he liked it, since he is a California dog. He loves to pose for pictures, and he loves riding in the car.

KOPCHAK, LISA

I have enjoyed photography as a hobby and have worked in the industry for over twenty years. Nature photography is a special interest of mine, but my favorite subjects are funny little canine faces. Mya is the newest addition to my "family," which also includes two other dogs, Missy and Max. We share a country home in Xenia, OH.

KOZEN, JANICE

This photograph was taken in a remote village in Guatemala. On this particular day, a religious procession was taking place to celebrate Easter week. I was fortunate enough to capture on film the feeling of mystery, sacredness, and purpose that those in the procession and those who lined the streets had. It was truly a transcendent moment. I have always felt that the best way to keep such moments alive and close to the heart is through photographs, with my camera lens being my best teacher when learning about the world. I plan to continue discovering these unique moments in other cultures for as long as I can operate my camera.

KREUZER, LOUISE M.

The maternal instinct is obvious in these beautiful purebred Australian shepherds. This is our mama girl, Lacy, embracing the youngest of her seven puppies, Makita, who was born on Mother's Day 1997. When they became old enough, I loved to take them out for a day in the outback—our backyard. It was so eventful! We love our hardworking yet playful Aussies. In addition to Lacy, we have Makita's dad, Shadow, and one of her older sisters, Aspen. They continue to bring us joy and amaze us everyday. Their hearts are full of love—unconditional love. Wonder if they're sending us a message?

KU, MADEAN

This photo is of my two oldest great-grandsons. They are brothers, ages $2\frac{1}{2}$ and 1 year old. We were at a tenth year anniversary celebration for our community care center. The boys saw the organ and climbed up to play on it. I had to take the picture because it was a different pose of them.

They like to play and do things together. Here, it looks like they know what they are playing.

KUHN, BRIAN
This photo was taken one early summer morning at the wharf of the Mayflower II, a replica of the boat the pilgrims sailed to America on. It is located in Plymouth, MA, "America's Hometown," where the photographer owns a marketing agency that produces brochures and websites for various customers.

KULIKOVA-BRAY, LARISA
This photo of my son, Savvaty, was taken while we lived in Vietnam and were stationed at the Russian air base on Camp Rahn. The photo was made at a Buddhist Temple near Nah Trang in South Vietnam. I always felt this was the best photo I had from our time in Vietnam. The name Savvaty is an ancient Jewish-Slavic name. It is also the name of one Russian Orthodox Saint, for which he is named. And now we live in Illinois with Savva's American father, James.

KUNZMANN, RICHARD
Using a Chinnon DP5 35mm camera with a 70-210 zoom lens, I took the picture "Spitfire, Snowbird Fly By" at the Abbotsford International Air Show August 6, 1999. This was the closing act at the airshow.

KYELBERG, CYNTHIA
This is a photo of my 13-month-old son, Nathan. He was at his grandmother's house. Nathan was amazed with the lit pumpkin his mom-mom, Betty Foreman, had made. Nathan has an 11-year-old sister, Amanda. I take a lot of photos of my kids, but this is one of my favorites!

LA PRES, GREG
The world around us provides pictures that change from one beautiful moment to another—similar sometimes, but never identical. I had this view for about an hour, catching only a moment of it for keeps. I left this untitled because I can't name the feeling I had as I lost my cares for the day and just relaxed there.

LADEMANN, JOAN
Tiger travelled from Florida to Long Island for a family visit and became our pet. Tiger was always in trouble, but with his personality you couldn't be angry with him. When left alone, he would open drawers and ransack them. His favorite toy was a sponge ball that he would always carry to the top of the stairs, drop, chase down, and carry up again. Tiger's life ended tragically when my husband, John, was cutting a tree down, and as Tiger watched, he was frightened by the chain saw and ran into the path of a passing car. After extensive surgery, we lost him.

LAKE, CASSY
During my summer vacation of 1999, I went to South Carolina to visit friends. I took a few days out of that trip to go with friends to Texas, since I have relatives there. The second day, my aunt took me to her in-laws' lake house on Lake of the Pines near Jefferson, TX. Around sunset, my cousins Phillip and Andrew and I went down to the peer. That's where I caught this perfect sunset

on film. Since I love photography, I take my camera almost everywhere I go, and it's pictures like this that make me glad I do.

LAKE, JANEEN
When I was taking this photograph, my friend, Erica, and I were on top of a boat. The waves were very large, so we were trying to balance ourselves in order to keep from falling. I'm not sure how the picture turned out as well as it did because of the movement of the water around us. While looking down the "Passage Through Land's End," I was amazed how peaceful it looked. The way the sunlight reflected on the water created such a contrast with the land around it. Vacationing in Cabo San Lucas, Mexico, was definitely a memorable experience.

LANE, CAROL
I am known for taking more than my share of pictures. My favorite subjects are my children and grandchildren. I am an artist and have fun gathering material for painting from my photographs. I also love the beauty of the Southwest. In my home, I have surrounded myself with its colors, fabrics, artwork, and artifacts. I was, and still am, so pleased with this photograph. It not only captures the warmth of the Southwest, but the warmth I feel for my grandson, Kelly, "Mi Amigo."

LANTZ, PAM
This is a picture of my two favorite fellows. Chester was 90 and Christopher was 4 at the time the photo was taken on the rails to trails in North Bend. Chester remembers when the trains ran, but Chris will know it as a bike and hike trail. I love to take pictures and have won a few contests.

LAPP, RON
I enjoy growing roses in our backyard for my hobby. As I watched this bouquet unfold in the house, I couldn't help but notice their beauty. As we admired their fleeting radiance, I wanted to capture this for all to enjoy—especially my wife. Using a rare sunny day, I set out to immortalize this in my photo. Several days later we further captured the everlasting memory by drying the "Roses" into a perpetual bouquet and still enjoy them in our home.

LARMOYEUX, PAT
On a sunny, breezy fall day, I took my grandson to the local pumpkin patch for some photo opportunities. He was, at first, anxious at the surroundings and then started to enjoy them when "something" landed on the side of his nose, producing the puzzled look in this picture. Though not flattering of my handsome grandson, the picture never fails to make me smile. I've always loved taking photos of my children, so with a new camera and a new grandchild this love has been renewed.

LARSON, R. D.
As a carpenter, I am always building other people's ideas, and I was searching for an avenue to express my own visions. I found photography enhanced both my work and creativity. This photograph was taken in early morning to provide a soft light and a natural dark background to enhance the depth of color, brilliance, and beauty of the lily, and thus was born "A New Day."

LAUNCHBURY, CAROLYN
My parents both passed away in 1999, my father on May 29, and my mother on October 27, after having spent their retirement years close to this beautiful seaside corner of the Mediterranean. The day this photo was taken, November 10, 1999, would have been their sixtieth wedding anniversary. That morning I went down to the rocks at daybreak to perform a sacred ritual to celebrate my parents' lives and their deep love for one another. The dawn that morning was magnificent, and I strongly felt their presence. I honor their memory with this beautiful moment in time.

LAWENDOWSKI, DIANE
I have loved animals my whole life, and I've made them part of my life, from doing volunteer work at the Humane Society, to working as a veterinary assistant for eight years, to starting and operating my own pet sitting service. Lil Bit and Patches, who are both 14 years young, are just two members of our pet family. A total of four dogs, six cats, six birds, and a rabbit share our home with us. I always have my camera loaded and ready and have an album full of pictures of our pets and those we take care of.

LEE, CHRISTOPHER D.
This picture was taken by my 8-year-old son while he was attending camp last summer at a building near Harbor Place in Baltimore City. I am his mother, and I was very surprised how well it turned out, so I summitted the photo in the contest.

LEHMAN, PATRICIA L.
For me, photography is an excellent way to express my creativity without excluding my family. In fact, I've found my children, Taylor and Calvin, have become my favorite subjects. In the process, I'm journaling their childhoods. In this photo, I tried to capture the curiosity that is constantly redefining the life of a toddler.

LESHKIVICH, KAREN
I am a veterinarian in Central New York and have owned, shown, and worked with bloodhounds for over twenty years. This picture was taken in Washington state, where Gibson and I were sightseeing after flying cross-country. Gibson is an active search and rescue dog and has assisted in finding many lost people; he is also a show and obedience dog and a companion.

LEVITO, VIOLA
This photo was taken on the bay at Long Beach Island. My friends and I sit and watch the setting of the sun; to me its the end of a perfect day. Nature photos are my favorite, as you can see, because of the colors and the peaceful time—a time to remember.

LEYVA, AGUSTIN A.
I enjoy taking pictures of unique moments. I took this photo of a unique child glancing out of a window of a two-story house in an alley near a market place in Lake Ochrid, Macedonia. I was fortunate to capture the eyes of an innocent child overlooking passersby. During a tour of duty in Europe, I took many photographs of interesting people and places. For a brief moment, I felt a sense of bonding through his eyes. I could not

pass up capturing this special moment. This child left a great impression in my life and proved that there is still innocence in this world we live in.

LIEMAN, RACHEL
This photo was taken the first time I visited Concord. In the summer, the area is crowded with tourists, but on this day in early spring we were the only ones there to enjoy the quiet beauty. I photographed the landscape on a whim and because my companions for this outing were tired of posing for me.

LISKOW, GEORGE
Mysterious, magical, and more, Antelope Canyon near Lake Powell in northern Arizona is one of many tributary canyons of the Colorado River carved by water over eons of time. As you enter this striking natural formation, you sense a presence, and you experience a Zen-like oneness with the world. My friend, David Boyd, and I spent an entire day there alternately taking pictures and standing in awe of the power of the place. As a destination for photographers or nature lovers, Antelope Canyon has few equals.

LONG, JOHN D.
There is nothing like a photograph to capture a special moment to be relived for years to come. Michael, 5 years old, played in the Amelia Island Youth Soccer League when this photo was taken. I took plenty of pictures at every game because I wanted Michael and his mother to always be able to look back at his first year playing soccer. This particular picture tells of a special child who always displays a can-do attitude and a winning spirit. I do not have children, but if I did, I would want them to be like Michael.

LORD, CATHERINE
This photograph was taken while on a tour of New England. When I entered the bridge and looked between the boards at the river, the sun shimmered on the water and accented the fall colored leaves of a tree on the opposite bank. The scene just asked to be photographed.

LORENTZ, BEN
My preference in photography is landscapes. I especially like to work with urban landscape, as I enjoy the eclectic mix of the old and the new architecture. With today's trend to raze the older structures to make way for modern steel and glass buildings, I feel that I must document the change. In twenty years, the buildings that we call modern today will be those set for razing. I see the city as an ever changing, viable, living entity. I work primarily in black-and-white and enjoy the challenge of taking that medium and transforming it into a thing of beauty. I feel that black-and-white photography brings about the stark reality that we call life.

LORENZ, SANDRA
This is one of my many photos of my dog, Friskie. We were on vacation in Florida, and everyone on the beach thought he was so cool! I frequently dressed him up for different occasions and he brought smiles to faces young and old. I'm sad to say that he recently passed away; but thanks to all my photos of him, his memory will live on, and he will live forever in my heart.

LOSURDO, DEBBY
This photo captures a very special moment for my husband, Robert, and I. We were on vacation in Hollywood Beach, FL. We were lucky to wake up early and see the most beautiful, romantic sunrise. Rob ran to get my camera for me so we could keep that memory forever. It was my birthday, and that made it extra special. I want to thank my father, Anthony, for all the wonderful vacations he took me on growing up. He inspired me to pick up a camera and capture every precious memory.

LOVE, WILLIAM R.
This photo of my cat, Misty, was taken in our backyard. Being a retired musician, I enjoy taking pictures. Several times I have been awarded "Yard Of The Month." Taking pictures of my home and pets has been my hobby. Erwin, NC, has been my home for thirty-two years.

LUCAS, PAM
C&O railroad was built around 1898, on Rout 60, east of Gauley Bridge, WV, to join main-line along New River. New River flows north from North Carolina. I have walked this bridge many times when hiking the tracks to fish. I have found etchings in rocks that I believe were chiseled by Indians. This place is described in James A. Thom's Book "Follow The River," a true story about Mary Ingles. Kidnapped by Indians in Virginia and taken to Kentucky, she escaped and walked back up this river. When walking the tracks, you can't help but think of her making this trek in the 1700s, when it was wilderness—like it is today except for the tracks and occasional train. In the left background is a hydro plant, which now supplies elkem metal, an alloy. Built from 1930-1935, it tunnels through the mountain three miles to Cotton Hill. Many lives were lost during the boring and afterwards from lung disease.

LUFFMAN, ALENE S.
My husband and I go to the beach every year for our vacation. Each time, I see something new and exciting about God's creations. This picture shows one of those fantastic views that God has made. I love the beauty of nature, the quiet still time of peacefulness, and the closeness to God you feel in a moment like this.

MACMILLAN, IRENE
My husband, Gordon, and I rescued Spike from the SPCA in Johannesburg, South Africa, when he was 3 months old. Before coming to America, we spent three years in Europe and traveled with Spike extensively. Here he is with Gordon in a ski-lift, ascending the slopes at Veysonnaz in the Swiss Alps. We have dozens of photos of Spike taken on our travels; maybe I'll publish Spike's scrapbook one day, but this one is a particular favorite. It captures the very essence of our much loved, globe-trotting canine companion, and Gordon certainly doesn't look bad either!

MADONIA, PAUL W.
On a trip to Washington, DC's, memorials, this man's derated stance moved me. He was immobile—as if frozen in a past memory on a soulful journey. Crowds of tourists possed him by; but he remained detached. Like a memorable photo, he transcended time, moved hearts, and captured feelings.

MANLEY, JUDITH
On this beautiful autumn "Day In The Woods" in Traverse City, MI, our granddaughter, Jessica, is depicted on a very cooperative fawn as the seasonal colors were changing. We were all like children that day. I was born in Montreal, Canada, and now live in Florida, where I specialize in special event management. I love to take photos. You might say I am a "click-a-holic." One of my favorite pastimes is making photo place mat collages of special events for friends and family.

MANSON, JUDITH A.
Meet Jessica Ashley. As you can see, the camera loves her and she continually kisses the camera back. I don't think it's possible to take a bad shot of her. She lives in Ankeny, IA, with her little sister Angela, who is three years younger and also a little doll. I am their proud and doting Auntie Juj from Los Angeles, and I am proud to say they were both born here, as was their father, my brother. Vincent and Karen most definitely have their hands full with these two. But Auntie Juj, amateur photographer on the move, plans on being there all she can to help out.

MARANDO, PALMIRA
This picture was taken by my son about three Christmases ago and includes me and my grandchildren Morgan and Keilee Knight, and Sierra and Ansel Bretz. I have other grandchildren: Alethia and Michael. I just turned 90 years old this past year on Washington's birthday, and people refuse to believe my age. Maybe it's because I have such a zest for living. I am in excellent health. I plan to live forever.

MARKERT, STEPHANIE
This is my beautiful chocolate Lab, Zo. The only canine thing about her is her breed. Next to my 5-year-old granddaughter, Jazmyne, she is my very best friend. On August 31, 1995, we spent the day at the beach. She swam in the ocean, ran on the shore with the wind blowing by her ears, laid on the warm sand soaking up the rays, and at the end of the day she stopped, bowed her head, and had a moment reflecting, "Boy, what a 'Dog Gone Day!'"

MARQUISS, GRACE
This is a picture of my granddaughter, Carly Rose. This was a very special time for me, as we live in Alaska and our son and family live in California. Visits are too far apart, and photos are a very important part of our getting to know Carly and her brother, Spenser. She had just slowed down after a very busy day of fun. The beauty of Alaska does not compare with the beauty of grandchildren and family.

MARSHALL, BETTY
This photograph was taken during a visit to my home state of West Virginia. I always enjoy traveling West Virginia's country roads in the fall of the year. The brightly colored foliage, the smell of the crisp autumn air, and the beauty, peace, and tranquility of the countryside are awesome.

MARTIN, JOSEPH
My 2-year-old son, David, is full of life, energy, and imagination. He loved wearing his helmet everywhere he went—including the grocery store

and church. On this warm fall day, David was enjoying an afternoon picnic with his family among the trees at Kanawha State Forest. I liked this photo because the leaves and natural sunlight cast a colorful background. David struck this Napoleonic pose with no prompting. His "sword" is a wooden letter opener.

MARZANI, SUSANNE
Eric is my first grandchild. He is 9 months old in this picture. It was his first Easter, and he was very anxious to get to Grandma's house to see what the bunny had left. His dad, Dave, was helping him get to Grandma's, while his mom, Amy, asked to see his license. At last they arrived, and the basket was full of goodies and lots and lots of love.

MATTHEWS, H.
This is my own work. It is a picture of my great-niece Toni Marie Matthews. Jim always played around, taking pictures of children and animals. This is the first time I've entered a competition. We have other children and great-grandchildren. Toni looked so cute, and I just had to take this photo of her. I'm a retired nurse. My hobbies are needle point and craftwork, but mostly I love taking pictures of unusual and interesting things.

MAUNE, GINGER
This is a picture of my daughter, Jamie Lee. In this picture she is 3 years old, and we were visiting family in Washington, MO. Jamie is putting on her father's cowboy boots and trying to stand up. She had tried several times before I snapped this picture. I was very pleased when I saw it, because seconds later she fell over. I have recently found a black-and-white picture of myself in my father's boots. I'm going to frame these two side by side and call them "Like Mother, Like Daughter."

MAY, BARBARA
This photo is taken in Grayland, WA, on the southwestern coast at sunset. I am an amateur photographer, and my profession is in aerospace manufacturing.

MCCARTHY, CHRISTINE
My best friend and I took a trip to California a few years back, and we went wine touring one day. We both bought a wine glass and one bottle of wine to bring home. I wanted a memory picture, so I set it up like advertisement. We drank the wine on New Year's Eve.

MCCORMICK, MAROLYN
I attended my first air show in September 1999, and was awed by the experience. I took this photo with the hope of preserving the exhilaration I felt watching the Blue Angels' performance. For the last eighteen years I have traveled between California and Montana, and being a grandmother with twenty-eight grandchildren and two great-grandchildren, I am never without my camera.

MCDONALD, KATHLEEN
This is a photo of my son, David Erickson, and my grandson, Sean. We live about five miles from the ocean. When my son was a youngster, I always took him to see the ocean—morning, noon, or night. Now that he is a father, he is taking his son to see the ocean. The picture shows so much love.

MCGILL, LISA
This is my daughter, Shelby-Lee. This picture illustrates Shelby's affectionate nature towards other children. Infants don't remain that way for long, so I take photos to capture precious memories of her that are rapidly passing in time. One day she is a newborn, and now she is walking and talking. My little girl is growing so fast that her infant days are just memories. This photo gives me the opportunity to remember the "Baby Love" she shared with me and others at the beginning of her life. I am glad I captured this priceless memory forever. Shelby-Lee, Mommy loves you!

MCGREGOR, GAIL
While visiting my daughter and her family in North Carolina, we made a day trip to Chimney Rock. When this natural wash down the mountainside to the river caught my eye, I asked my granddaughters Danielle, Jennifer, and Stephanie to sit, and I took this shot. The images provided by nature and never cease to amaze me. I got several great shots that day.

MCINTYRE, CHRIS
This photo was taken on a trip I took to Albuquerque, NM. We had been on the road for three days from New Orleans when we arrived. Within hours of our arrival, it began to snow. Everyone joked, saying that I had brought the snow with me from Georgia. The next day we woke and drove to the mountain peak. The picture is of an October sky that took my breath away. I'm thankful to have captured such a moment in this picture.

MERRIHEW, ART
While living in Alpine, TX, before moving to Colorado Springs, CO, I would witness beautiful sunrises and sunsets. At the time I took this photo, there was a forest fire in the mountains, causing the sun to glow in shades of red. I climbed upon my stepladder to wait and shoot over the trees, and in waiting for the timing of the sun to set with my zoom lens, I was able to capture "Evening Sunset."

MERTENS, LINDA
Upon glancing at the shaded window, the first thing I noticed was the green eye and the blue eye staring at me. She seemed to almost become part of the lace shade—a mosaic of sorts. Little did I know when I adopted my "Diva" from the animal shelter, she would become such a priceless work of art.

MESSINA, GIANNI
This photo came about as my wife, Amy, and I were showing the sights to her sister, Lynn, who just arrived from the Philippines to visit. At Cypress Garden in Florida, with all the beautiful things to see, I looked down at the water's edge and saw this beautiful white egret with bright yellow feet standing so "Tranquil" on the cypress tree.

MESSINA, JOE J.
I've been an avid photographer for over twenty-five years. I've won a couple of photo contests locally and obtained some significant recognition.

When traveling, I carry most of my equipment and have been nicknamed Fast-Finger for my frequent shooting and desire for the right location. Most images are lost by either waiting too long or not taking enough time to find the proper shooting location. Some of my best photos are of animals and pets—especially my rabbits. In this photo, I captured a special security and serenity in this one's freedom to come and go through the opening in the cage.

MEYERS, GERRY
This is an image of my grandson, Daniel, wearing his "Boone hat," as he called it. We were at Eldorado Park, and he looked so cute in his red shirt and hat that I told him to go over by the tree so I could take his picture. This was the image I liked best.

MICHAEL, LINDA
My family is the most important thing in my life. Capturing them on film is a passion of mine. This is a photo of Madison, my only grandchild so far. She is the only one that doesn't run and hide or tell me to put the camera away when I start taking pictures. Right now, she loves posing for the camera, and I'll keep taking pictures until she too runs and hides. Maybe by then I'll have another grandchild!

MILLER, MITZI
This is a photo of my daughter, Sierra. She was a little over 2 years old when this picture was taken at her grandmother's house in Hustontown, PA. Sierra is always into something, and our family is always ready with a camera to catch the memorable moment on film so it will last a lifetime to share with everyone.

MILLS, ELISE R.
This little 5-week-old bundle came to us three years ago, found abandoned at a Rose Auto store near our home. It was Saturday, and I was cleaning when I realized I had not seen the puppy for a while. I must have looked in all her puppy places for fifteen minutes when I finally looked up, and there she was, all cozied on the couch between pillows. This was definitely a camera moment. My husband, Guy, and I have two other dogs, Lady and Duchess. The bundle is now as big as the couch, and her name is Rosie.

MOBLEY, VIRGINIA GAIL
This photo was taken on my birthday in 1999, and I saw a whole new world beyond the dark clouds. I felt so at peace—like I was the only person on earth waiting for God to open the golden sky of awesome wonder and let me in. This is how "Awesome Wonder" got it's name. It was awesome, and it made you wonder what was beyond there.

MOORE, ANNE KIMBERLY
This photo is of my very special kitten, who will forever live in my heart. She was a sweet, spunky, and cute kitten. My sunny kitten brought joy to my life when I needed it most, as I was about to have major back surgery. Although I will never hold her in my arms again, as she succumbed to blastomycosis, she will be forever alive in my heart. I will always cherish the memory of her in my heart. We named her Gizmo from the moment we saw her black and white, funny face. If cats go

to heaven, then I am sure Gizmo must be there among the angels.

MOORE, ELEANOR

I have traveled throughout Scotland, finding the ancient monuments the most fascinating. When the wind blows, you can almost hear the voices discussing the daily events. How did they build these magnificent structures so long ago? When I arrived at the Calanais Standing Stones, a cross-shaped setting of stones, the timing was perfect for this picture. It looked like the rainbow emanated from one of the stones. This site was buried by peat nearly 3,000 years ago, resulting in the unique markings on the stones. The stones were built from 3000 B.C. to 1000 B.C., abandoned at about 800 B.C., and excavated in 1857.

MOORE, KENNETH AND FETTA

Our photograph was taken at the Indiana Dunes National Lakeshore, Mount Baldy in northwest Indiana. This area demonstrates outstanding impressions of nature at its best. The fall season, in both of our opinions, is like looking through a kaleidoscope. The radiating rainbow of vibrant colors seem to invite you to explore the wonders of nature. That day, we had taken many pictures of very impressive sceneries. However, we both felt that of all the pictures that we took, we had not captured the ultimate scene. We were about to end our tour of Mount Baldy, when miraculously, simultaneously, our eyes migrated to the most breathtaking and panoramic scene of the day. Our only objective at that time was to capture that moment in time. So, I positioned our camera just right and took the most beautiful picture of nature that we had ever seen. After we had the film developed, my wife was so impressed with the picture that she painted a beautiful oil painting of it.

MOORE, PHYLLIS DAVIS

Born and raised in Martinsville, VA, I moved to the mountain state in 1976. Because my son, RL, is an avid outdoorsman, he has taught me to appreciate nature. My favorite seasons are spring and fall. I take advantage of any opportunity to take pictures. "Eye Of The Beholder" was taken on an outing in the fall of 1999, to see the changing of the leaves and to behold the awesomeness of God's handiwork.

MORALES, SARA E.

Kimberlee, my 2-year-old granddaughter, is holding Stephanee, my 3-day-old granddaughter, as Candise, my daughter-law, holds them. Richard, my son, is the proud father looking behind the scenes as I am taking the picture. I live in Columbus, GA. I was visiting my son, Richard, while he was stationed at Fort Polk, Louisiana, as an Army nurse. I am now retired, and my hobbies include crafts.

MULLIKIN, WILLIAM E.

This photo is of our rottweiler, Sammy, kissing our schnauzer, Smokey-Boy, and at the same time shaking hands with a family member. Sammy and Smokey-Boy like to play tug-a-war. Sammy seems to know he is much larger than Smokey-Boy and always lets Smokey-Boy win. Most people think rottweilers are so mean, but I'm convinced it is all in how they are raised. I don't take

pictures often—just on holidays or special occasions like this. This photo shows how kind and loving rottweilers can be. Love and kindness does wonders for people and pets.

NAGY, GABRIELLA

My love for nature started at my childhood. I admire the slightest detail of a petal or leaf, the soft pillow-like clouds on the azure blue sky, and the artistic design of the wings of a butterfly. Being an animator, every movement in nature—from a gracefully gliding seagull, a trotting horse, or a dancing flower in a summer breeze—amazes me and fills my heart with new wonders each time. To capture one of these moments of this wonderful, mysterious world is both an honor and a delight.

NEDEAU, DANIEL

As I was watching the ship glide by Margerie Glacier, I noticed how the sky was clearing up over the mountains. I positioned myself on the stern of the ship, and I patiently waited for the ship to get into position for the perfect clear shot of the mountain. This is a product of Fairbanks Mountains, Glacier Bay National Park, AK, from the deck of the cruise ship, "Jubilee," on September 25, 1999. My wife, Denise, and I love to travel—especially out west among the mountains. We love to share our experiences and photos with family and friends.

NEFF, JOSEPH J.

Photography has been my hobby since buying my first camera in grade school with newspaper route earnings. As a private pilot and world traveler, I always have a camera with me. I have made visits to every US state and twenty-five countries primarily because of business as a now semi-retired chief engineer and also for holidays with my wife of forty-two years. This photo of a mother lioness and baby was taken on a January 1999, photo safari to Kenya and Tanzana. The lions were photographed in the Sarengetti National Park. Low vision from glaucoma has required me to adapt to use my right eye instead of my now-damaged left eye.

NGUYEN, HUNG

This picture was taken in the summer when the sun was going down. Within the work of art, the sunset came and showed the truth in peace. The mother and her son were coming back after the long working day selling food. That image is in my mind, and I will never forget the loving and caring between the mother and the son.

NIEBERGALL, PATRICIA

I took this photo of my grandson, Cameron, at his home in Salem, OR. He loves being outside in the garden. He is the light of my eyes and is the subject of many of my photos. I keep my camera near at hand for photos of my family and friends. My husband and I travel quite a bit, and I love capturing all of our memories on film. I like to think that my love for the subject shows through in the photo.

NIELSEN, SOREN

I am a graduate student from Denmark studying biochemistry. During a study visit to San Diego, CA, my wife, Lisa, and our two sons, Mikkel and Rasmus, and I were fascinated by the spectacular

hummingbirds and butterflies. On our trips we tried to carry our camera with us as much as possible in the effort to capture some memories of these magnificent creatures. This nearly two year stay in Southern California produced a lot of pictures, many without any bird or butterfly. However, a few turned out to be worth all the effort.

NOBLE, ROSEANN M.

This photo was taken after a severe storm in Texas. It was during a time in my life when I too was going through a storm—a storm of cancer. During my recovery, my husband, knowing how much I loved taking pictures of the clouds, would always take me riding, and I would take lots of pictures observing God's handiwork. On this particular day, with the clouds still moving across the sky, dark and luminous, I felt at peace. I didn't know why, but I knew something had changed. My pain was gone, and I began to feel strength within. After arriving back to our son's home, this feeling continued to linger. I rested while my husband took the film to be developed. A few days later when he brought the pictures to me, I was looking through them, and to my amazement this picture, "Christ In The Clouds" was there staring me in the face. The joy and excitement that filled my soul was overwhelming. I realized that the feeling of peace that had overcome me was God's confirmation to me, letting me know my sickness was not unto death. He was then and is still watching over me. Praise be to God!

NOEL, FRED

Our pet dog, Scamper, is a little rascal. Whenever I use my flashlight, he will grab it and run around the house with the light beam shining on the floor. I decided we needed a photograph of him. It was difficult taking the picture because he always wanted to lead the way. It reminds you of an usher in the movie theatre showing you to your seat. Our children are grown and married, and our grandchildren really enjoy it when we give Scamper the flashlight.

NOLAND, DUSTYN

This is a photo of my son, Dustyn. We were on vacation and Dustyn was enjoying the view from our motel room balcony. I couldn't resist getting a picture of that cute pose. I love to take pictures of Dustyn, and I thought this one really captured his beautiful blue eyes.

NOVICKE, MARGUERITE

Marguerite is known in South Jersey as an artist, interior designer, gourmet caterer, and photographer. She actively supports young artists and she is active in her community politically with economic development. She studied at Philadelphia College of Art and Fleisher Art Memorial and Tyler School of Art. Both are in Philadelphia.

O'CONNOR, KAREN

As a photographic hobbiest, I prefer taking spontaneous, unposed photos. But I couldn't resist this one when my daughter plopped my grandson down among the pumpkins to get out his bottle for lunch. Ever patient, Jake just sat and examined the pumpkins while waiting. As an only grandchild, he'll soon get used to a camera pointed at him every chance I get.

O'DONNELL, JAMES R.
This bridge connects Cincinnati, OH, and Covington, KY. The bridge was constructed by John Roebling of Brooklyn Bridge fame. The image was taken from the twenty-ninth floor of a building. I used a Canon EOS 1N, and Canon 100-400 IS zoom lens, set at 300mm. I stopped down to f22 to get the star effect on the lights, and this resulted in a twenty second time exposure on ISO 400 Royal Gold film. Besides the star effect, which I really like, you can see the streaked white and red lights of the automobiles going across the bridge.

ORGERA, CIVITA
I like to take pictures of flowers that I grow in my garden. I love to capture their beauty in full bloom. This particular flower I grow indoors. I named it "Night Beauty" because it blooms only at night and only for one night, for by morning it is wilted. Through the years I stayed up many nights watching it bloom. It is a spectacular sight to see the petals open slowly into a burst of beauty and fragrance. It does not bloom often, but when it does, it gives me great pleasure and a wonderful feeling.

ORLANDO, BARBARA
My granddaughter, 21-month-old Cheri Lynn, was waiting patiently for the evening show to start at the Polynesian Cultural Center in Oahu. I quickly snapped the shot when I saw her hands in her pockets. I didn't realize her expression until the picture was developed.

OSBORN, PHYLLIS A.
This is a photograph of my granddaughter Madeline's first pair of shoes purchased only days prior to her first birthday, which she proudly wore for all to see. At this writing, she's now 18 months old, and this pair has been retired. Although she now has more than one pair of shoes, there's something very special and sweet about the "First Pair."

OWEN, ZERITA J.
There is always beauty at the Central Oregon Coast no matter what the weather. The young man in this photo wearing a wet suit and holding his surfboard is watching and waiting for a fellow surfer. The ever changing ocean and solitary figure was too tempting to pass up. I really enjoy photography but have much to learn.

OWENS, LINDA
The most exciting things happen in the sky, and I love to take pictures of them when I see something special. This extraordinary sunset could be seen from my deck, and I ran for my camera to catch it at its peak. It occurred over the Oquirrh Mountains in Southwestern Salt Lake City, UT, near Kennecott Copper Mine, formerly known as Bingham Copper Mine, which was first discovered by two of my great-great-uncles. My husband, Bill, and our children, Lesley, Carrie, and Tyler, also love to see the beautiful sunsets from our home.

PAGE, ALICE
I've loved to use a camera all of my adult life to shoot anything and everything, but I shoot mostly nature subjects. However, this is a photo of my tiny great-grandson, Collin, at 4 weeks old and five pounds. "After A Yawn," he always gets this startled look of round eyes and pursed lips and would seem to be thinking, "What was that?" He and his identical twin brother, Ayden (who doesn't make this face), give me plenty of opportunities for photographs. They live with their adoring parents near lake Tahoe and, I'm sure, will someday become wonderful skiers also.

PANCAKE, PATRICIA
My husband, his sister, and her husband and I spent a week's vacation in Maine exploring the countryside. We made several roadside stops each day, camera in hand, trying to capture the autumn beauty and animal life and especially hoping to find a moose. This picture was taken at dusk on the last day of our trip. We returned home with many delightful pictures, but none of a moose.

PANKRATZ, DOROTHY
This is a photograph of Daniel George Pankratz, my grandson, and my son Dave's son. I snapped it during a visit to my daughter's house in Riverside, CA. I brought the dessert. Luckily, I brought a lot of it. The party consumed two crates of strawberries that evening! His middle name, George, which he was named after my father, is appropriate since (among other things) Great-grandpa George was a strawberry farmer back in Wisconsin. A grandson is one of life's blessings! Strawberries are another of life's blessings!

PARKER, ARLENE
I saw the natural beauty and drama around me and decided that what words cannot describe, the camera captures forever. Most of my pictures are taken within a mile from home. I can stand in the same place and take a picture each day. They are all different. This wasn't started as a hobby; it just happened in the last five years.

PARKER, JENNIFER
Not everyone's journey through life is down such a peaceful and charming path as displayed in my picture. I wanted to capture this image so that everyone could see how peaceful a journey life could be if it is looked at from the right perspective. As you walk through this life, just imagine these birch trees watching over you.

PARRETT, BARBARA
This photo is part of our ritual in getting our "kids" ready for the snow they love to romp in. The caption was inspired by the expression on Cookie's face, the Sheltie-mix, who has been through this many times before. Mandie, the poodle, also knows what is happening. On the other hand, Corkey is new to us and very eager to pose for us and show off his new coat. Hope (the woman in the picture) and I have many photos of our "family." It was very difficult to choose our entry from our many keepsakes.

PARSONS, JENNA
I have always appreciated a beautiful sunset, and this one especially caught my eye. I took this picture in Wilmington, NC, in September 1999, after Hurricane Dennis and before Hurricane Floyd hit. I am a technical communicator in Research Triangle Park and rarely have the opportunity to capture such an expressive vision.

PAZIK, GLORIA
This photo is of my son, Scott, at the age of 2. Scott's grandpa, "Bumpa," as he called him, always said, "The reason a person gets sleepy after eating is because your stomach and eyelids are hooked together!" He passed away in 1998, but seeing this photo always reminds our family of his comment and, in turn, brings many other memories to us.

PECK, RACHELLE
I took this picture at a boys' and girls' club in Knoxville, TN, for my photography class at the University of Tennessee. I volunteered at the club and had the opportunity to spend a few hours a week with some of the sweetest and most energetic kids I've ever been around. This particular child loved attention and always ran up and gave me a hug when I walked into the club, so I decided to take this picture one afternoon while he was playing.

PEDIGEAU, MERRILEE
Among the lions, tigers, and bears (oh, my), I met this playful lion at a nearby wild animal refuge. Like any youngster, all he wanted to do was play. Being an animal lover, most of my photographs are of animals, birds, and the outdoors. Of course, my special favorites are of my personal cats and dogs. Photography is a way of capturing that special moment—that look, that feeling—and keeping it near our hearts forever.

PELLOT, ELBA CRUZ
My name is Elba. In this picture are my son and my first grandson. They live in Puerto Rico. It was the first time my son came to Puerto Rico with him. I was so excited; I wanted to capture every move the baby made. I saw him making this funny gesture with his face, and I just had to capture it on film. I didn't even know it was going to turn out so great and funny.

PENNER, CHRIS
Hi! My name is Chris, and this is my dog Yoshi, who is an akita, a Japanese breed. We were playing tug-of-war with his favorite toys, old socks and towels, when all of a sudden he stopped, sat down and stared at the television long enough for me to get the camera and snap this photo. I am single, live in Fargo, ND, and own my own business. I'm very excited about having this photo selected for publication. Thanks to all involved!

PERFETTO, DORIS K.
I've been a photographic hobbyist for years. Although I've been to Colorado many times, this was my first trip to the "Top Of The Rockies." My husband is on the right, and our good friend Kevin is on the left. The limo we had rented with three other couples made a spectacular turn around on the narrow road of the Continental Divide, where this picture was taken at 14,000 feet above sea level. This was a day of spectacular sights we will never forget.

PETERSEN, HARRY
This mother possum was in a field near my home.

She was so loaded down with her babies, she couldn't run away from me. I always carry a camera with me in my car. This allowed me to not only observe this rare sight, but to be able to photograph it. I was raised as a farmer and now I am a sales representative for a petroleum company based in southern Michigan. As a family, my wife, Marlene, our daughter, Cindy, and our sons, Mike and Mark, along with nine grandchildren share a deep and genuine love for Mother Nature and all her gifts.

PETERSEN, PAM

My daughter, Laura, and I enjoyed "kindergym" together in the fall of 1985, when she was 1½ years old. Watching her wait impatiently for her turn on the trampoline was precious. I saw her smile transfer into sheer delight as she realized just how high she could fly on the trampoline. Soon after shedding her diapers, she joined the local gymnastics club. Today, in the year 2000, Laura is 16 years old and a high level gymnast.

PETERSON, MARK L.

This photo was taken from my favorite Chicago location. On this particular weekend after Chicago Bears football legend Walter Payton passed away, I was so moved by the tribute I saw in lights bestowed by the people of Chicago to our fallen hero that if not for my tripod mounted camera, I could not have taken this photograph. My heart pounded and my hands and legs shook. Rest in peace, Walter Payton.

PETHERBRIDGE, ANNE

This is a tribute to my father. He not only gave me my life, he taught me the importance of independence as well as perseverance, loyalty, and dignity. Thanks, Dad, for everything.

PHILLIPS, CYNTHIA S.

Growing up near and living around the water provides so many opportunities for beautiful photography: sunsets on the bay, ships sailing in the gulf, and pelicans perched in curiosity on their posts. The water has a calming effect on me and in photographs. In this photograph taken in my boat at Weeks Bay near Fairhope, AL, I encountered a curious pelican that seemed to enjoy posing for the camera. I believed this angle to be his best side. I also enjoy photographing various scenery, historical landmarks, portraits, and individual requests such as personal homes.

PHILLIPS, KAREN L.

I peer through my camera at the shoreline, anxious to preserve our vacation along Cape Hatteras National Seashore. Buddy, our Bichon Frise, is sitting slightly in front, with me on a reclinable beach chair. I try to absent his head from the viewfinder, looking for that scenic picture that says what I feeling. As I'm perusing the seashore, I catch a glimpse of his expression. Posing mesmerized and serene, an ocean breeze romances him, ruffling his woolly fur. Quickly, I change perspective. Using the scenery for background, I focus on a portrait of our dear Buddy. He is saying it quite well!

PINKERTON, JAN

This is a photo of our first rottweiler. He was 8

weeks old at the time the picture was taken. My husband, Mike, and I have two other dogs, and they are all our "babies." I cherish this picture, since it captures the "Little" Colonel as he was as a puppy. He is now full grown and looks quite different, but he still is as adorable as he was in this picture.

PORCH, ROBERT

I began photography after I won a $5,000.00 Fellowship Grant from NJSCOA for oil painting. I also become a member of International Freelance Photographer Organization. I'm a self-taught visionary abstract artist, and my motif is a Divinor of light. The paranormal photo coexists to accompany an autobiographical novel of 600 pages, plus a global overview of fourteen years. I'm aiming for film, TV, and international markets. My influences are contact from an Angelical being in the sign of a geometrical flowered 3-D cross with a heartwomb-matrix center on September 12, 1970. An unclear organic earth garden sacred dynamic fruit, or possible outside incert purple ray spectrum, the other.

PORTER, J. C.

This is a photo of my granddaughter, Jessica, at 4½ years in our backyard. I am a single grandpa who has taken care of Jessica since she was 5 months old. I love taking care of her and enjoy many things with her. With the help of family and friends, I hope to watch her grow up and be a beautiful person.

POWERS, REBECCA W.

My brothers and I host the Hayes-Litton family reunion, started by our father, John Hayes. The year 2000 will be our twenty-fifth year. My brother Ronald Hayes is playing the puppet. Pulling the string is ventriloquist Nathan Radford. Ronald is an identical twin to Donald Hayes, who is responsible for getting Nathan to entertain the children and the rest of us. Nathan is a Christian ventriloquist who provides wonderful, refreshing entertainment in this day and time. I enjoy taking pictures, and am thrilled to share this one, which portrays some of the fun we have each year.

POYNTER, PEGGY

I never got tired of looking at this picture I took many years ago of my son, Kevin. It always makes me smile when I think about the little boy that stood still long enough to have his picture taken with Candy, his best friend.

PRESTON, VIRGINIA

Don't be fooled by the apparent calm patience of this shih tzu puppy. At the time this picture was taken last fall, Bandit was only 5 months old and was not agreeable to being dressed in clothes, nor sitting still for the camera. The reason this picture is so amazing to me is that I placed him in the doll chair and then quickly stepped back to snap a picture without having time to aim. With his face turned towards the camera, it's easy to see that he has one blue eye and one brown—thus his unusual name.

PUCKETT, VIRGINIA

This is my great grandson, Mitchell, who is 2. He didn't think anyone was watching. I love taking

candid shots, and I thought this was a cute one. I am retired from banking, love to travel, and take snapshots for memories.

PULLIN, LINDA

My husband, Domingo Galvan, came up with the idea for the picture of our son, Desie Ray Galvan, when we were taking pictures of him for some outside fun. We wondered what his thoughts were. With a mirror in front of him, could he see the innocence and beauty that we saw? We also figured in the future he could see the past of our fathers, and how they got ready for Saturday night dancing. Memories are great, but a picture preserves the past for the future generation.

QUINT, ROSE

Photography has been a hobby of mine for about twenty-seven years. I always have a camera with me ready for those special moments. The beauty of the sky can always attract my attention. I've always worked indoors, so when I'm out, I really appreciate nature. I live out in the country and there are always beautiful scenes to shoot. My other hobbies are softball, bowling, and computers. I am also an active volunteer at a women's center. I have a very supportive husband, a wonderful son and daughter-in-law, and one very active grandson.

QUINTO, ANNE M.

It was my very first time visiting New England in the summer of 1999, and I happened to drive by this unique-looking post office in the beautiful state of Rhode Island. Myself being a postal employee from San Diego, CA, it was only fitting to coin "Got Mail?" as the title of this photograph.

RANSOM, TERESA

This photo was taken while on vacation at Atlantic City. I'm not a picture taker at all; it was just one of those pretty sights that make you say, "Ooh," or, "Ahh." My husband, Craig Powel, who is a NFL player, was driving, and I took the shot. I was amazed how pretty the picture came out. Craig and I both are amatures at taking photos, but we just had a little baby girl and taking photos now is second nature.

REIFENBERGER, JUDY

This photo gives people a feeling that everything will be getting better. About a forth of a mile down Cornell Road, property was damaged by the tornado that hit on April 9. Apartments, homes, school property, and our nature preserve were all hit. Having traveled this road to work at Sycamore School for nineteen years, I found it very hard to travel after the damage was done. One morning I spotted "Big Bird," and it just gave me a feeling of peace and made it easier to travel. Big Bird was there until frost came!

RENAUD, PAULINE

This picture has given me much pleasure. It was taken during a week spent in the Precincts of Canterbury Cathedral last summer as part of the Berkshire Festival Chorus. The emotional and spiritual impact of living in essentially two different worlds was a lasting one. In addition to the photograph, a poem bearing the same title is being published. Faith, music, and poetry have always been important aspects of who I am. My week in Canterbury incorporated all three, providing a unique and incredible experience. I am pleased to have added this visible reminder through photography.

RENAUD, PHILIP S.
I really enjoy taking pictures of animals—especially of my dogs. Each have their own personality I try to capture on film. At the time this photograph was taken, Micki was senior of my two other dogs. His role as their mentor and his intelligence inspired me to create this setting. It also compliments Micki's natural ability to make people laugh. I hope that others will share the warmth and humor this photograph has given me and my family for years to come. That is the gift of photography.

RETHERFORD, TAMMY
Our family has been in the produce business for over fifty years, so I thought this picture would be appropriate for our announcements. We specialize in watermelons, and the melon in this picture is one that we raised. Our business name is Melon Man, and my husband, George, is known as the melon man. Megan is 3 days old in this picture.

REYNOLDS, LINDA E.
I have many hobbies—flowers, cats, remodeling old houses, and small landscaping—but the most relaxing is photography. I take pictures on paper like paintings on canvas. I like pictures where you can walk into them and feel like you're there. As I was walking one morning, I couldn't resist taking this picture of the sun coming through the trees and the points making a cross. Feeling the breeze on your face and smelling the mist was just breathtaking.

RHINEHART, ANNE
I guess I caught my "shutter-bug" from the mother who constantly used a Kodak Brownie at all family functions. I'm forever shooting people, places, and things. This shot of the iris is a bonus; after dividing my iris bed and giving extra to our neighbors, there were still leftovers. My husband said, "You can't throw those out," so he planted a whole row in the vegetable garden. The result was so beautiful that I couldn't resist. I was so pleased with this artistic photo that I had it enlarged for our daughters to frame. Thanks for appreciating it too!

RINGER, LISA M.
This photo was taken at Cogshall Park, which is located in Fitchburg, MA. I remember going to the park as a young child to swing on the playground, feed the ducks, and enjoy the beautiful surroundings. The gazebo was a popular spot for band concerts and wedding photos. Hopefully this gem will be around for years to come so young and old can enjoy!

RIZZUTO, GINA M.
My mother, Cindy Michel Rizzuto, realizes the importance of capturing special and once-in-a-lifetime moments. Gina, 9, her brother, Anthony, 2½, and Honey, our pomeranian, are hams for the camera. Cheese!

ROBERTS, SHARON J.
This is a picture of my daughter, Lesli, on her wedding day, October 9, 1999, with her nieces and my granddaughters, Katie, Kellie, and Kacie Crain, as her flower girls. I was able to capture the adoration they each have for one another. I enjoy photography and always try to capture a natural moment to create a beautiful memory.

ROBINSON, BLAKE
This is a picture of my son, Blake, modeling his first raincoat. Blake was 2½ years old when I took this picture. His great-grandmother Eunice Hooter sent him the raincoat for Christmas. The photo was taken so that she could see him dressed in his raincoat. I love to share pictures of my son with other people. I don't think that you could ever have too many photographs of your family. This one will be treasured forever.

ROBINSON, LYNN
This photo is of my son, Colby Robinson, and his dog, Lady Bell. Colby is 2 years old and loves his dog. Colby helps Ma take care of her. He enjoys playing with Lady Bell, but Lady Bell is old and slow. Colby tells her she's a good girl. This photo is special to us. We can look at it and see how much Colby loved his dog. Lady Bell is gone now, and this photo has memories I wouldn't trade for anything.

RODRIGUEZ, REHINA
This photo was taken three days prior to Hurricane Lenny, which struck the Caribbean in November of 1999. This storm came at an odd time in the hurricane season. The cloud formation fascinated me at the time, so I took the photo. I like capturing nature in the wind as its beauty unfolds around us—a message from our creator.

ROGUS, VICTOR
For many years I have worked honing my skill as an amateur astrophotographer. My work has been published in International Science Magazines and even on a cd-rom. My love for photographing the night sky often leads me to the darkest places I can find, where my cameras will not be disturbed by the glow of city lights. Sometimes it is very cold, and sometimes I am served up as dinner for millions of bugs; but the beauty of God's universe is one that I cannot resist documenting. My photograph of Saturn and the moon was made on September 18, 1997.

ROLANDER, CRAIG
On July 4, 1999, a severe windstorm and a series of tornadoes hit the area known as the Boundary Waters Canoe Area Wilderness in northern Minnesota. Millions of trees were damaged or knocked down. This picture was taken three weeks after the storm. Although the area has been changed, the beauty of the wilderness remains. Special thanks to my wife, Dawn, for her help in planning this trip.

ROUSE, DEBRA ANN
A camera is my companion. Everyone always expects me to take photographs. Year-round, I enjoy enclosing memories in the form of photographs in notes to friends and families. "Lunch In The Park" was photographed in Philadelphia's

Rittenhouse Square. A kind gentleman feeds his friends, the birds, individually by name. As a child, I watched my father develop black-and-white photographs in our basement. I inherited a natural talent from a man who has mastered many trades. I'm married, I've earned a B.A. in public relations, and I now work happily as a sales administrator. My hobbies include snapping candid shots, shooting billiards, singing, and biking.

ROY, MARY
This is a photo of my 4-year-old daughter, Kristy. She enjoys growing her own pumpkins; she especially likes watering them. I asked her if I could take her picture with the pumpkins, so she went over, sat down, and put her feet up. Kristy likes the fall season for the colored leaves, pumpkins, hay rides, and Halloween. She lives in Maine with her mom and dad. I take a lot of photos to capture special moments that I want to keep forever.

RUNZA, JOSEPH G.
Maria is the oldest child in a family of migrant workers. Each summer they come up from the Texas border to West Michigan to work in the fields picking cucumbers. The photo was taken at one of the migrant camps where Maria and hundreds of other children spend the summer with their families during the picking season. She is a wonderful subject—unassuming, shy, and completely unaware of her own beauty—yet typical of the children of the migrants who work our fields each year.

RUPE, GREGG
This is a photo taken on the first morning of our vacation while my family and I were on the balcony, waiting for the sun to rise. We have been to two other beaches, but this one was different. I learned how to use a camera in 1988. Now I carry a compact with me most of the time. I like sunsets also. Every week there is a different color and sky pattern. Nature provides a wide variety of pictures to be seen. Being there at the right time with a camera is the challenge.

RUSS, KENNETH J.
I love to photograph what Mother Nature provides. This beautiful scene was shot in the early morning at Arches National Park, UT. I have been photographing the western states for over fifteen years. There is no greater pleasure in the world for me than capturing on film scenes like this for other people to enjoy. God created this beautiful planet called earth that we are blessed to live on. Please enjoy its gifts of beauty and always remember to bring a camera.

RUSSO, JEAN F.
This is a photo of my two grandchildren, Katilyn and Zachary, on a trip with Gram to Yankee Kingdon to build their own scarecrow and visit the pumpkin patch to pick out their pumpkins. I love taking photos; my mom had so many pictures, and so do I. It is so nice to be able to look back and see everything.

SAMMARTANO, MARY
Cats, being naturally playful animals, provide many entertaining moments. This photo of Christie was taken in my enclosed Florida room. I often photographed both her and her sister, Agatha, so I

was lucky enough to have the camera ready to catch her in this unique position. I did not see the butterfly until after the picture was developed. A timeless moment never to be repeated.

SANDERS, NANCY K.
This antique stove is still in use in a lakeside cottage in Michigan that belongs to a friend of mine. It has faithfully provided meals and memories for generations and represents one of many sources I use for my paintings, which decorate my home and save history for my family and friends to enjoy forever.

SANDRONI, MARK
When I first entered the contest last year, the big subject was the upcoming crossover to the year 2000, and the thing on everyone's mind was what would happen to the computers. So I felt the best way to commemorate the 1999–2000 turnover was a picture made completely of gold computer chips. Happy millennium.

SAUDER, VERNON L.
You never know what might happen when you close your eyes to pray! This took place at my brother's wedding. Austin Beiler, the ring bearer, closed his eyes for prayer while Bailey Tiemersma, the flower girl, decided it was an opportune time to give a smooch. I peeked and couldn't resist capturing the moment.

SCHEINBERG, MARY
My great-granddaughter, Kaylx, was amazed that Opie could say her name and tell her he was "a gorgeous bird." Opie whistled the Mayberry tune for her. They had a mutual admiration that was heartwarming to watch. I have eight other great-grandchildren—Benjamin, Chloe, Zackery, Kimberley, Kristie, Bryant, Billy, and Jessica—who love to come visit Opie. Two toy fox terriers—Bambi (she bounds like a deer), and Trey (he has three spots)—complete the menagerie they play with on each visit. The animals and bird seem to enjoy the visits as much as I do. The interchange between the children and the pets that love them is an ongoing pleasure to me and gives me many wonderful memories.

SCHELL, LOA M.
Photography has always interested me. I thoroughly enjoy capturing unusual and phenomenal sights and sharing with others who were not as fortunate as I was to observe the spectacular moment. Dust storms such as the ones in Phoenix, AZ, are experienced only one other place in the world: the Sahara Desert. This truly is a masterpiece of its own.

SCHLEFSTEIN, JILL
This photograph is of my 4-year-old niece, Jamie. She is simply the most beautiful work of art I have ever seen. It is hard to take a bad picture of something so beautiful. A modeling agency wanted some photographs of her; they said I could just take some pictures myself and send them in, you do not need a professional photographer to take them. So I broke out an Olympus zoom-lens camera that I stole from my sister and started snapping. I haven't put the camera down since. I think I may have found my calling, finally.

SCHMIDT, DEBORAH
When my sister and Ramses' "mom," Darleene, and I decided to vacation at a cabin in the wilds of Maine to hunt moose with cameras only, we stopped halfway at a hotel. Ramses spent the first hour standing on the hotel bed admiring himself in the mirrored closet doors. He was finally coaxed off the bed when, because we had forgotten a can opener, room service came with his canned food served on a bed of lettuce complete with garnish and a silver cover.

SCHRECK, JOSEPH D.
Born in western Kansas and reared in the Dust Bowl days, I developed eagle eyes for whatever beauty of nature there was to be found: including "snake" flowers, cloud formations, and sunsets. As a Capuchin Franciscan, I learned to see the signature of God in all of nature. One night while offering Mass at the base of Cerro Morales, I saw the moon above the silhouetted peak. Breathtaking! I etched it on my memory, never dreaming to reproduce it with a camera or on canvas. Finally, forty years later, I captured that hauntingly beautiful scene on film.

SCOLARO, MARY L.
This photo is not only a breathtaking view on a beautiful day in Florida, but a total look of love and devotion between man and man's best friend. Grandpa Gail, my brother, is retired navy. Buck is the Great Dane in our family; and he belongs to Gail's daughter, Charlene, and Bill and their three children. Buck has given our family joy and lots of laughs. He has his own "bunk bed" in the master bedroom. Our family pets have special places in our lives. This photo was taken at a family birthday gathering in September 1999, at Buck's home.

SCOTT, CLARA
I am an amateur photographer, and I love taking pictures of everything. My husband, Bob, and our two sons, Marion and Aron, said that I should take it up as a career instead of a hobby. When I saw "Pointing Guard Rockey," I thought he was so cute pointing. When he hears something that he does not understand, he will point and hold his right paw up until he sees what it is and where it comes from.

SCOTT, JENA
I love taking pictures. My husband, Garek, says that I take too many! This photo of our daughter Emma was taken in August 1999, at Venetian Gardens, which is the park where Garek and I were married in 1995. I brought Emma there for a photo shoot. She is 20 months old in this photo. I was six months pregnant with our second daughter, Madeline, when I took this picture. Since Madeline was born, she's had her own share of photo sessions—both on her own and with big sister, Emma.

SEMONES, ANNA
These beautiful Blue Ridge Mountains of Virginia are near perfect for finding a lookout to view the beauty God has created. Whether it is from this lookout standing at an overlook, or just driving the Blue Ridge Parkway, one can feel the stress just fade away. Come to Virginia; you won't be disappointed.

SERRANILLA, IMELDA I.
I took this picture during the summer season in the country. The first thing I said to myself was what a green! After colorful leaves fall comes snow. After snow melts comes attractive flowers. After flowers wither comes green, and I saw greens everywhere. They are full of strength and always standing all year-round, always in bloom no matter what the season is. They were full of life and full of hope. I am a photo hobbyist who always wanted to capture scenic beauty like these trees. They are my inspiration and provide nourishment for the soul.

SHAIN, KENNETH
Signal Rock in Woodmont, CT, is a favorite location for young people for swimming and driving throughout the summer months. This historic landmark, pier, and former civil defense beacon on the Connecticut coast is seen in all its glory during a great New England blizzard. Having summered there myself throughout the '50s and '60s, it gave me a great joy to share this location with my three sons the summer before this picture was taken. Amazingly, this picture was taken the first time I had ever seen my old childhood haunt in the winter.

SHAW, JACKIE
This photo of my 3-year-old granddaughter, Jenna, captures her view of life. She truly enjoys everything she does, and her enthusiasm is contagious. Being with her always lifts my spirits.

SIAKOOLES, ECHO
I have had cats all my life. I love all animals and love taking pictures of them. I have dozens of photos of my pets. Friends have often asked me why I don't submit some of them for publication. This photo of Daisy is my very first effort to do so. I am very pleased to think it has been accepted.

SILIS, KEVIN
I love to take pictures—especially of wildlife and all that the outdoors has to offer. While on this trip to Kootenay National Park, the last thing my wife and I expected to photograph was a timber wolf, yet here was this gorgeous creature allowing us the opportunity to enter its world, if only for a brief time. We spent an intense and enjoyable twenty minutes with this wonderful creature. We felt blessed to be able to experience the presence of one of nature's most wonderful accomplishments. It is an event I wish everyone who loves nature could experience.

SILVA, AUDREY
I took this photo just as the sun was setting and dark clouds were rolling in from the Texas hill country. A placid, yet ominous photo, it captures the intensity of the sudden thunderstorms that frequent the Lone Star State. My favorite subjects deal with the beauty and vitality of nature and the quiet intensity of open environments. A California native and Texas raised, I also enjoy painting and have a passion for living. I reside in Garland with my two feline forces of nature.

SIMMONS, BECKY
This is a photo of my only child, Christopher, just exploring and enjoying life. He passed away in

1997 at the age of only 21. I have many pictures of CW, and all show precious, beautiful memories! I love you, CW. —Mom.

SINCLAIR, SHERRIE H.
Coming from an illustration background and working as a Disney animator, life experiences and observations serve as valuable inspirational resources to me. One such moment occurred in a Paris Cafe where, between mouthfuls of a tasty mushroom and cheese filled crepe, I couldn't resist, (dog-lover that I am), pausing long enough to capture this engaging slice of Parisian life as a French patron addressed his pet at the bar. I enjoy taking photos such as this not only for reference purposes, but also as another avenue of artistic expression and storytelling, using black-and-white film as a means to focus on composition through shape and value.

SLACK, SHARON J.
Being a grandmother and great-grandmother, most of the subjects in my attempts at photography are naturally related to me or my pets. My husband and I share our home with a Doberman pinscher and two cats. However, while standing in the St. Louis station waiting for a train to take us sightseeing, I looked through an arch and saw this magnificent view of the arch. Not being a great photographer, I didn't expect much, but I just had to try capturing the dramatic light and shadows there before me.

SMITH, ALVA P.
This is a photo of my uncle, Hura, bottle feeding one of his pigs. This was on his farm in Mississippi. I took pictures whenever I visited. I thought this was rather unique. I was a special education teacher for twenty-eight years for the Los Angeles County Board of Education, and now I am retired. On January 22, I celebrated my seventy-fifth birthday. I was married thirty-eight years when my husband passed away in 1985. I have lots of photos; it was difficult for me to choose.

SMITH, BETTY J.
I am a widow, and my son, Rod, one my five children, lives with me. He and my granddaughter, Katrina, persuaded me to take two very small 4-week-old kittens. Our very big dog, Buddy, welcomed and tried to care for the kittens when they arrived. I take many pictures of my family, my cats, and my dog and at my church. Rod's hobby is woodworking, and he had to get into the lumber pile and disrupted the cat's favorite place! This day, Tiger decided to crawl into the pad, and I snapped his picture. The family loved it!

SMITH, BEVERLY
I'm always taking pictures, and this was the first chance our family had to enjoy a weekend in the outdoors. We were up in the Citrus Forest in some hidden caves in the woods. As we reached the bottom, I took this picture looking out from the cave. It was like a whole new world to "Escape" to.

SMITH, DIANE
It was a great day for picnics. As you can see, the clown had visited our picnic at Franklin eagle 2309. At center stage was Etta, who was having a great time. Her co-pilot on the right is Joyce.

Queen Marty is staged behind Josh,who just had his face painted. I took this candid shot on the spur of the moment. This picnic was the first time our pilot, Etta, had been able to enjoy herself since losing her longtime friend, Tim. The balloons cheered her up and we all had a great day.

SMITH, KISHA
This is a photo of my daughter, Kiarra, enjoying her bubble bath. I just had to capture this Kodak moment. As you can see, she would not smile for me, but the picture was developed quite well with her adorable little self. Mommy and Daddy love you always and forever, "Angel Of Mine."

SNECK, GARY
This is a photo of Tiffany Hakkarainen and one of her kittens. Tif is very much an animal lover. She is also a best friend. I've been taking pictures for some time, but I've just now started to study the art of photography and learn what a camera can do. The more I learn about the art, the more exciting and interesting it is, and the better photographer I become. Photography is work, fun, and a little bit of luck.

SOKOLL, ANNETTE
This photo was taken when my children spotted this bird on the side of the road by our cottage. I always have my camera by my side. The bird posed for me in the woods. I have been going up to our cottage since I was 8 years old and never had a bird pose for me like this one.

SOUZA, SANDRA L.
This picture was taken in the marsh off Duxbury Beach, MA. After approaching and taking several pictures, I was later informed by the harbormaster that it is not uncommon for seals to beach themselves for up to two tide changes. They like to rest also. I carry a camera at most times to capture moments like this.

SOWINSKI, PATRICIA
This photo of my nephew, Eric Ian, was taken the day of his mom's wedding to his new stepfather. Eric is a sweet, charming, energetic kid, but on this day, he was mad because someone else was taking his mom's attention away from him and he didn't understand why. I felt so sorry for my "Little Peanut," and I tried to cheer him up; but, as you can see from the look on his face, he was still upset. Needless to say, he has since adjusted and is happy and adorable as ever. I will love and cherish this little boy forever.

SPENCER, ROBERT F.
On that early spring day, my wife, Nettie, spotted Hashbrown on the garage roof. The cat belongs to our daughter Shannon. I ran for the camera to photograph the cat after he had jumped and landed on the birdhouse. Does he think he's a squirrel? We know he's a little nutty!

SPOFFORD, JOAN S.
I have always enjoyed capturing on film my family, my friends, special occasions, ane even some not-so-special occasions. My den shelves are lined with albums that tell the story of their enclosed photos. So that we could be closer to our only living child and her family in Atlanta, we

moved from Pennsylvania to a senior community in South Carolina. On their first visit, our son-in-law, Hank, decided it was time to share the sport he loved with his 2-year-old son, Henry. Thus, the photo "First Lesson" was made. Since then, Henry has acquired his own golf bag with a putter and a "long shot club" (his sister's term), plus a green plastic golf cart. He begins his telephone conversations with, "Grampa, when can I come to Sun City to play golf with you?"

SPORER, STEPHENIE
This is a picture of our only daughter, Stephenie, in her original pumpkin costume.

STAGGERS
This is one of our favorite photos of Missi Lou and Miley Roy, affectionately known as M and M. They are most often the subjects of my picture taking sprees. The stress of any day simply disappears when we come home to these guys. They bring us so much joy and give us an endless supply of unconditional love. Who needs Comet and Cupid with Missi and Miley in the picture?

STARK, ELIZABETH
This is a photo of my nephew Peter, age 5, on Christmas morning. He was trying to hide in a group of stuffed animals. I got my camera and took about five pictures. This one came out the best. I love the expression that he has.

STAWINSKI, DEANNA
This is a photo of my dog, Cujo, when he was 9 weeks old. He is almost 9 years old now, and I have just found out he has bone cancer. Even though his time is now short, I still look at him and see the little puppy sitting in his toy box, guarding his toys. He has been a big part of my husband's and my life. He has been our protector, our companion, and our friend. We will miss him, but we'll remember him always and all the joy he has given us. We will celebrate his life!

STEELE, NORMALEE R.
My husband, Virgil, and I were working in our yard when I noticed several frogs around the pond all in the vicinity of my cement frog. I ran, got the camera, and snapped away. Once developed, it seemed natural that they were paying homage to the "Frog God," as my sister, Donna Lynn, had called my cement frog. My three children, Johnson, Evonne Marie, and Steven, are always telling me to stay away when I have a camera in my hand. But, needless to say, I love to click away, taking photos of anything standing still.

STEELE, SARAH
I am a graphic designer, but my love for art spans across three mediums: photography, graphic design, and oil painting. I love photography for the instant shot I can get. Luckily for this barn, I got the shot before it was too late!

STELLEK-BROWNE, JAIME
My occupation as a figure skater has taken me around the world. I learned very quickly to appreciate the gift of a photograph. A photograph is a memory of a lifetime. Although sometimes a hassle, it pays to carry a camera at all times. You never know when opportunity will be right in

front of you. This photo was taken at sea world in Orlando, FL. As this crane posed so prodigiously, I felt as if it was saying, "Hurry, Take The Picture." I dedicate this photo to my parents, who have always supported me in whatever I do.

STEVENSON, BRIAN L.
I am employed by the Department of Public safety as a fish wildlife protection trooper and I have enjoyed the opportunity and good fortune to have lived and worked in numerous small communities in our state. Alaska's grandeur is such that around every corner it provides unparreled beauty for all to enjoy. We currently reside in the interior part of the state surrounded by the Alaska and the Talkeetna Mountain Ranges. The fall photo is of Fishcreek on a clear crisp day, allowing the sunlight to radiate and enrich the colors.

STIGER, MARILYNN
I am a nurse and was just returning home after working a night shift, when the sun was just coming up. The combination of the heavy dew and sun produced the fabulous picture of the tedious work of a busy spider.

STIGERS, JASON C.
This picture was taken on my honeymoon with my lovely wife, Holly. We purchased the camera that took this picture the day before I took it. We could not have asked for a more rewarding gift to ourselves. We've always enjoyed photography, but never expected to have been at the right place at the right time to have captured such a breathtaking photo. This will add another fond memory to a wonderful honeymoon.

STOLP, BARBARA
This picture was taken at a birthday party my husband and I gave for the grandchildren. One was born October 30, and the other was born on November 19; they are eleven months apart. One of my most favorite things to do next to singing is taking pictures. The best pictures have been those developed from a moment that I took the time to see the gift.

STONER, GLENN E.
The members of my immediate family all have cameras, but my son Glenn II has the real talent for photography. I carry a camera whenever I am traveling, hunting, fishing, or just four-wheeling. When I see something in nature that catches my eye, I just snap a shot of it. It's just amazing how beautiful, different, and interesting our world is if only we could take the time to enjoy it. That is how I took the picture "Chuska Mountains." Thank you, Ces.

STRAIN, LA DONNA
This photo was taken about ten miles outside my hometown of Cleveland, OK, in a town called Hominy. The idea was inspired by my daughter, Cortney, who shares my love of photography. The Indians are steel cut-outs that appear life-size from a distance. I would like to dedicate this photo to the memory of my dad, Benny Goodwin, and my mom, Donna Goodwin, who continue to support and challenge me. I love you.

STREIFEL, MARGUERITE
This photo was taken last summer as I visited the place of my birth on the Spirit Lake Reservation of Fort Totten, ND. The purple cone flower grows with great profusion on the prairies there. The healing power of this flower, echinecea, is well known to many. For me, the healing was not just restricted to the roots of the plant. As I lay in that clover field gazing on the beauty of this wildflower, I also experienced an inner peace and healing as I contemplated the beauty of these pink partners nestled in the prairie's vast expanse.

STUMPF, JANE
On October 8, 1999, our daughter, Cheyenne Raine, was born. We were thrilled at the way Savanna, our cat, took to her. In this picture, Cheyenne is being protected by Savanna. Daddy says they are his "Two Babies."

SUNDY, AILSA FAYE
I've enjoyed taking pictures since my husband bought my first 35mm camera eighteen years ago. We usually take our vacation time to visit our daughter and grandchildren in South Carolina. The south is so beautiful that all you need is a camera and click away. We were riding around and saw this beautiful old church, and I just had to stop for a picture of it. I'm really happy now that I did, because someone else saw the beauty that I found that day in this old church.

SWEENEY LILLIAN, LILIAN V.
I was driving through Lexington, MA, on a beautiful day, and I came across this lovely area with colors so vivid. I just had to take a photograph of this vibrant and beautiful scene of fall foliage. This scene is about half a mile from the Minute Man statue in historic Lexington.

TANG, THIEN
This is interesting. I came back in my country, and when going to the countryside area, suddenly I saw an old lady with an unruffled expression on her face. She seemed to have accepted reality in life, and I admired and thought that: "A happy of the me."

TANSKI, DEBORAH
This is a photo of my great-niece, Jessica. I called Jessica's name out so she would look at me when I took the photo. I didn't see the expression on her face until I saw the picture. Whenever I take photos of a subject, I try to take three or four photos in the hopes that one of them will come out good. I love sharing my photos with family and friends.

TARTAGLIA, SARAH BETH
This photograph marks the beginning of a new chapter in my life. Although I have studied photography throughout the last seven years of my life, I have never looked at it as more than a hobby until now. It took the love of a very special person in my life, my boyfriend, Bobby, to bring about the inspiration and confidence I needed in order to realize and pursue my dreams. "Woodland Wonders" is one of the first images to arise out of this very special relationship. I am honored to be given the chance to share the beauty of this unique, fantasy-like image that is by far one of our favorites.

TESSMAN, BERNICE
My husband, Bob, and I are retired. We took a bus trip to the New England states and to Canada during October 1999. I enjoyed taking pictures of different types of subjects and especially scenic photos when we arrived at Niagara Falls. I thought they were beautiful, and after looking at them I turned around and got the panoramic view of the bridge with the fall colors. It was awesome! I knew I had chosen the right one from so many different beautiful photos when my husband choose the same one.

TESSMANN, JERRY
The mystery of nature overcoming the past is just a matter of time and not always doing things fast. Some things in life you learn to live with. Some things you just grow attached to. Some things just end up in knots. The scar will remind us of one moment in time.

THOMPSON, CAROL
This was my dog, "Bandit." He was my best friend and companion, and he lived only to be 5. Though that was young, he had a rough beginning. At birth the breeder tried to drown him and put a cigarette hole in his hind end and in the back of his head. How could someone be so cruel to a 4-week-old puppy who weighs only eight ounces? He was so small I had to bottle feed him. I believe he felt I was his mother. He was very small even in adulthood. He was the love of my life, and a hole has been left that will never be filled.

TINLEY, EMERY B.
I picked this Bugs Bunny photo because it shows him just the way he is in his cartoons. This was the Macy's Thanksgiving Day parade. It wasn't that easy because I had the Pink Panther, Spiderman, and Woody Woodpecker to choose from. But since Bugs Bunny looked so much taller than the others, I chose him for that particular pose. I love these types of pictures in addition to landscapes and seascapes. That will be my next venture, I hope.

TODD, BETTY
The photo is of our grandson Adam Bice and his grandfather, Gilmer Todd. His grandpa was asked to watch him for a few minutes, and you can plainly see what happened. We have two daughters and three more grandchildren. Our daughter Renee McCumber is the mother of Charlie and Megan. Our daughter Bettina Dixon is the mother of Adam and Ansley. We are very proud of them. My hobby is counted cross stitch. I give away more than I keep. We are retired and enjoy life with our grandchildren.

TOLAND, CHERRY L.
Eventually all things do meld into one. My love of the outdoors and fly-fishing lend to great opportunities for photography. Alaska certainly rates high on the list. How fortunate to spend the day photographing grizzly bears and live to tell the tale. I managed to take so many pictures that it was hard to choose. I felt "Bear Necessities" was truly a once-in-a-lifetime photo. He was a great fisherman; however, catch and release was not on his mind. We have already planned a return

trip. There are too many fish left to catch and pictures yet to take.

TOLEDANO, MARA

It was a sunny November day while I was walking along the beach. I aimed my telephoto lens toward a seagull and took the best photo I have ever taken. It was very rewarding when I saw the photo for the first time. It came out so good! I had more snapshots of the seagull with its head up. I thought this one with its head tucked under its wing had out-done all the others. It's even more rewarding to be able to share my favorite photo with the public.

TRANUM, LINDA

My appreciation of nature probably began in childhood when my parents, Bill and Dorothy, built a house on the Pennsylvania countryside where pastoral scenes and animal life were plentiful. For me, this was a magnificent learning experience. I shot this photo at the Berlin Zoo in Germany when this lovely polar bear couple captured my heart. I believe humans have become arrogant as we think the earth is ours to do with as we please while many of our animals are becoming extinct. We must learn to have true reverence not only for human life, but also for plant and animal life.

TREPAS, DONNA

From my snowy back porch, I saw this beautiful scene. It didn't look real with clear crystal hanging from trees. I enjoy taking pictures of beauty that I also hold in my heart. I share these pictures with others so that they too can see the beauty of our world. My camera goes everywhere with me for fear I might miss something spectacular and it would be gone forever. I am a substitute teachers' aid in Picturesque Pagosa Springs, CO, where I take pictures of our beautiful area. Each picture has a life of its own, and this life is mine.

TROHA, KATIE

This picture was taken on a fifth grade field trip to Greenfield Village in Dearborn, MI. My friends and I wanted to take this picture because it's not every day you get to lay down on a railroad track. The train went by the night after the picture was taken. My friends and I had an awesome time, and that is why whenever I look at this picture, it brings back great memories.

TURNER, JOY

I was adopted from the SPCA on February 27, 1997, and was named Lucky by my dad, who passed away on September 12, 1999. My mom loves and spoils me, and I give her many hours of enjoyment. When my mom returns from shopping, I got through all the bags until I find my new toy. Besides my toys, I have more snacks than the grocery store. I just got a new baby sister named Penny Panda. We play and have a good time together. Asleep or awake, I am truly living in a dream world.

TUTERA, KIMBERLY M.

There are so few precious moments in our lives when we realize the true innocence of existence. However, that quality is best animated in the actions and explorations of a child. Thanks to over a decade of devotion to children, I embrace every opportunity to capture moments like these to treasure and cherish for eternity. Many more thanks to my fabulously creative mother, Marlene, for reminding me to always maintain my youthfulness and for inspiring me in my photographic pursuits.

TUVI-UTHE, MARIE

I was raised in France and studied designing, tailoring and history of costumes through the ages. After coming to America, I studied and went into the world of "beauty" at a salon where I display my work. Always with an eye on taking photographs wherever I go, I took this picture near Dana Point, CA, after an afternoon boat ride. Since I am always with camera, I was ready for this great peaceful moment at sunset on the way back to port.

UMPHLETT, CAROLYN

I've always loved taking pictures of family, friends, and our pets. Sometimes it is really fun when they are caught off guard. I told my husband, Wayne, and my daughter, Leslie, that Chance took my son, Frankie's, bed because he wanted to meet Santa. So, we took a picture of him. I'm glad we got this one, and I'm glad that it will be published in a book because my daughter loved Chance very much. He was very special to her and the rest of us as well, but in July 1999, he got very sick and we lost him. Of course, we have our pictures and memories, but this happening makes my daughter and the rest of us so happy because his memory will live on forever.

VAIL, KIM

This photo was taken on the Vail Farm, where I live with my husband, Craig, and two daughters, Erica and Abby. It was taken in the fall of 1999, while working on a school project with my daughter Abby. The colors in the sky during the fall months were breathtaking. I took several pictures, and Abby selected the ones she wanted for her project. I decided this one was too beautiful to tuck in a drawer. This photo has captured a small part of God's creation displayed in a colorful sunset. It reminds me that through him "Anything Is Possible."

VALENTINE, CAROLYN

What a cat! Leo was cat, dog, and person. He loved most everyone, and they loved him back. If everyone had his disposition, it would be a great world. He checked outdoor noises like a dog and consoled like a person with a paw on each shoulder and his head against your cheek. Your lap was his haven also. I love taking pictures, and many people say I take good ones. I also love animals and people. I have had seven cats over many years, and all were loved. Leo hated to see certain people leave, and he would stand or lay on your feet as long as he could.

VAN SICKLE, RON

This photo is of my cat, Ashley, and was one of my first pictures taken on my Olympus OM-1. I was hunting around the house looking for subjects when I caught her soaking up the sun on our bed next to the window. I love this photo because she has such character in her eyes. Pure contentment.

VAUGHAN, OCTAVIA

I always aspired to be a photographer, but the truth is that I rarely take pictures. This picture was taken with a disposable Kodak camera purchased especially for my trip to Yosemite with the hope of capturing some of its beauty on film for memory's sake. I submitted this picture simply because it received so many compliments. I'd like to close by saying: "The heavens declare the glory of God; and the expanse sheweth the work of his hands" (Psalms 19:1). This picture is a beautiful display of God's handiwork, and I thank him for gifting me to take it.

VIERRA, GERALD

My wife and I retired to Flagstaff, AZ, in the summer of 1998. After thirty-three years of working and raising three children in the midwest of Kansas, we moved to the scenic serenity of 7,000 feet. We enjoy the tall ponderosa pines and, of course, the wonderful color of the aspens. The air is pure and the mountain water is naturally chilled. As like the golden aspens of autumn, my wife and I are in the fall golden years of our lives. We enjoy taking snapshots of family and only recently started taking photos of nature. I feel a moment captured on film is a lasting and historical account of what our time on this earth was like!

VUONG, KENNY

This is a farmer's job after the harvesting season. They are unlucky in life and must adjust to working hard only by hand. I want to keep a record of some of the activities in my country after my trip.

WALAT, MICHELE

I have loved photographing the beauty of our Creator since I was a little girl. The animals especially have such a sweet innocence and a beauty that is almost inspirational. This is my cat, Marty, who I rescued from an animal shelter when he was 3 years old. I caught him relaxing in a sunny spot on a cold winter afternoon.

WALES, DREW

Jesus said, "You shall enter the Kingdom of Heaven as a child." This photo of my daughter, Danielle Grace, reminds me not only of her beautiful bubbly spirit, but the beauty of children that is a gift from God. I serve as priest at St. Michael the Archangel Charismatic Episcopal Church and live in Rockledge, FL, with my wife, Julie, Danielle (a teacher), and sons Joshua and Peter Michael. Our oldest son, Jayson, his wife, Jennifer, and my grandson, Jonathan Drew, live in Maryland.

WALKER, JENNY

This picture was taken on our farm. On that early spring day, the light at that particular moment was just so beautiful that I couldn't resist a shot. The scene just seems to pull at you, begging you to be still from life's busyness. I enjoy taking pictures of nature's beauty and wonders in my spare time.

WALLAT, LIDONNA

I enjoy taking pictures of animals. It is very relaxing to watch animals use their freedom. I found out if you take the time to enjoy the pleasure of life, and see what they have to offer, you can catch about anything that they want you to see. You just have to have patience.

WANJURA, ELIZABETH

To me, taking pictures is just plain fun. It's an easy hobby to get into when you have such precious things to photograph. My niece loves to play dress up and have her picture made. My nephew also loves playing and getting his picture taken. I was taken by the seriousness in their faces as he examined her baby. I hope that the two of them always have the closeness they share now. I hope they always know they have a special place in my heart and that I love them more than chocolate!

WATTS, TRACEY

This is a special moment we wanted to remember forever while on vacation at the Outer Banks of North Carolina in July 1999. Our son was 8 months at the time, and he still loves his Nana as much today as he shows us he does in this photo.

WEBER, LAURIE

I have always had an interest in a beautiful settings as well as a great love for children. This photo was taken in Lacrosse, WI, when we were moving back to Georgia to reunite our family. I opened the suitcase to fill for the movers to take later, and, to my surprise, I found my daughter. There had been a lot of confusion, and Erica had chosen a quite, safe place to rest. But she didn't want to be missed or forgotten during the move, so she appropriately selected the suitcase.

WESSEL, MARY

This is a photo of my first great-grandchild. He is now 3 years old. His mother is Victoria Randolph, and his grandma is Sylvia Randolph. He loves to have his picture taken. His birthday is March 4, 1997. His name is Dylan Michael.

WHITE, ELIZABETH P.

This is a picture of our dog, Dakota, at Mill Creek Park in Youngstown, OH. Dakota was a pound puppy but became the little prince of our house real soon. He just loves going to the park and playing "King Of the Mountain." This $35.00 dog is priceless to us today.

WHITE, MARJORIE J.

This is a photograph of my German shepherd, Logan, and it is especially dear to me now because Logan is no longer with us. I spotted this field of daisies growing along a highway, and, fortunately, Logan was with me and so was my camera. Getting good pictures of animals involves a great deal of luck, being in the right place at the right time, and having a special subject. I had all of those when this picture was taken.

WHITFORD, RICHARD F.

In the fall of 1999, I was returning home from a trip to the New England Baptist Fellowship and a Maine church speaking engagement about the Gleam Mission's ministry. As I was driving along admiring God's beauty, I went down a steep hill and into a valley, and looking over to the left, I saw this picture. I continued going out of the valley up the hill and just could not get this picture out of my mind. Something told me to go back and take that picture, so I turned around, and went back. Am I glad I ever did. I also have a horizontal shot, but this was better. As I dwell on this pic-

ture, I can't help but think that it was God that created this picture, and I only recorded it!

WHITNEY, LISA

My husband, Michael, and I could hardly wait to buy our first home so we could start a family of animals! Sam, our blue-eyed, flame-point manx kitty; Chena, our husky-malamute beauty; and our appropriately named huge malamute, Moose, have brought so much joy and laughter to our lives. Needless to say, It was a difficult task to only choose one photo to send in, so I chose my mother's favorite. Chena is outside, looking at her reflection in the window while Sam is trying to play with Chena's tail. They still play that game to this day!

WILHELM, CHARLES E.

This is a photo I took when on leave. I was stationed in Germany and decided I wanted to see Italy. This is one of several I took, and I have always cherished this photo. Being a frustrated artist all my life, I plan to paint this in oils or acrylic now that I have retired, and I plan on enjoying the fall and winter of my life.

WILKINSON, EVA

Our granddaughter, Carria, 8, and our neighbor Mary, 92, share something special: a friendship that spans the ages.

WILLIAMS, BERNARD A.

This is a photo of my fiance, Barbara J. Brockenbrough, taken on Valentine's Day 1998. Our love was always in full bloom the entire 4.8 years we had together. Her mother, Janice Fitzer; her daughters, Lisa and Joanne Guevara; her granddaughter, Whitney Barnes; and son, Eric McKee; and I miss her beautiful smile very much. She passed away January 20, 1999, at 11:15 A.M. I will never forget her last pulse. Our love will remain in my heart forever. She was my life, my joy, my all.

WILLIAMS, IRVIN

This is a photo of a friend of mine. Her daughter goes to college in Japan, and she sent this fan to her for her birthday. I gave her the nickname Hotshot a long time ago, so that's how I came up with "Hotshot In Japan." I live in Jackson, MA. My hobby is photography.

WILLS, MICHAEL LEE

The basis behind this photo and what I was trying to present is a look into what is considered by people to be beautiful or ugly. I feel in blending these two elements, something very extreme and vivid can be brought about. I think if we as people look at things in a totally different way, we can then accept and embrace the differences of ourselves and others. I find that something beautiful can be found in things that are considered ugly or disturbing. I am attracted to things or people that possess a strange otherness.

WIX, ANNE

I've taken many photos of my purebred Tonkinese cat, Debutonks Valentine Bliss, but this picture of Bliss asleep with the sunlight and shadows is one of my favorites. Bliss is 7 years old and was a twenty-fourth wedding anniversary gift from my

husband. This picture was taken in a garden window in our former home in Delaware. We now live in sunny Florida where Bliss and his companions, Azura and Mocha, have many sunny windows in which to nap.

WRIGHT, BARBARA A.

The fall morning dawned cold with an unexpected snowfall. This peaceful scene greeted me across my back deck in beautiful Maggie Valley, NC. Knowing it could quickly change, I put on bedroom slippers, grabbed my camera, and stood on the snow-covered deck to capture the moment. Ignoring my very cold feet, the serenity I felt left me with a warm and contented heart. What a wonderful moment in time! Beauty is indeed in the eye of the beholder. "Beauty is truth, truth beauty, that is all ye know and all ye need to know."

YOUNG, ALLEN

This picture was taken in 1975 during my third tour of duty in Vietnam with the corps. No matter how Americans felt then or now about the war, this picture represents the basic right to obtain freedom—a right that, unfortunately, Americans take for granted.

YOUNG, SISSIE

My handsome husband, Roger Young, rescued this baby long-eared owl when it blew out of its nest in Monument Valley. The first two nights he had it, the mother came by and dropped prepared food for the baby outside the tent. Roger created a habitat for the little guy and named him Hollywood. He trapped mice in the horse feed for food and helped the owl along with his natural instinct to hunt. By throwing Hollywood in the air, the owl became strong enough to fly. This story has a happy ending too, Hollywood was reunited with his mother and flew away to freedom.

YOUNG, VALERIE W.

Not only are they best friends of their masters, but Buster and Pal, mixed German shepherds, are best friends of each other. Buster was 2 years old when Pal came on board. There was much concern about how well one male dog would take to another male dog. Buster turned out to be the best "mother" a new puppy could have ever had. This picture was taken in the hopes of capturing the love and trust they have for each other.

YOUNGBLOOD, CYNEVA

There is so much beauty around us if we will only take the time to notice it. You can make a conscious effort to look for the essence and, therefore, develop an appreciation for the beautiful things in life. Our days will seem a lot less harried, as beauty has a way of totally capturing our senses, making us forget all our troubles in life, and for a brief moment nothing else seems to matter. And the wonderful thing about capturing beauty on film is that we can store it forever. In our minds and hearts, the beauty will be always with us.

ZAHARKO, HARRY K.

This summer photograph, captured during a very early morning hour, was taken as I was going about my work duties on the golf course I am employed with. That particular morning was extremely foggy. Because I keep an old 35mm camera with me, I was able to be at the right place at the right time. This moment only lasted less than ten minutes before the orange light disappeared!

ZYLKA, COLEEN

I am taking pictures all the time. When our daughter, Cameron, came along, I couldn't take enough pictures. One day she was crabby, so I thought I would try taking her 6-month-old picture. As you can see, it doesn't matter how bad your day is—you can always look at your children and truly see a basketful of joy.

INDEX OF
PHOTOGRAPHERS